MW01152999

VOLUME 45

MIKOYAN GUREVICH
MiG-21 FISHBED

YEFIM GORDON and PETER DAVISON

specialtypress
PUBLISHERS AND WHOLESALERS

COPYRIGHT © 2006 *Specialty Press*

Published by
Specialty Press Publishers and Wholesalers
39966 Grand Avenue
North Branch, MN 55056
United States of America
(800) 895-4585 or (651) 277-1400
www.specialtypress.com

Distributed in the UK and Europe by
Midland Publishing
4 Watling Drive
Hinckley LE10 3EY, England
Tel: 01455 254 450 Fax: 01455 233 737
www.midlandcountiessuperstore.com

ISBN-13 978-1-58007-106-2
ISBN-10 1-58007-106-6

All rights reserved. No part of this book may be reproduced or transmitted in any form or by any means,
electronic or mechanical, including photocopying, recording, or by any information storage
and retrieval system, without permission from the publisher in writing.

Material contained in this book is intended for historical and entertainment value only,
and is not to be construed as usable for aircraft or component restoration, maintenance, or use.

Printed in China

Front cover:
The Ye-5 prototype differed from the Ye-4 in the engine installed. The Ye-5 was powered by 5,098 lb-st AM-11 power plant, which boosted the top speed by nearly 700 kph (434.9 mph). The Ye-5 was unveiled on 24 June 1955 and NATO assigned the reporting name Fishbed to the prototype. (RSK MiG)

Title page: The Ye-6U/1, first of the two-seaters. (RSK MiG)

Back cover:
Top: The low-altitude performance and takeoff and landing performance of the F-7E used by the "August 1" Aerobatic Flying Team for flight presentation are improved because the double-delta wing and leading edge maneuver flap are employed. (via Yefim Gordon)

Middle: The export F-7 IIA fighter was produced by the Chengdu Aircraft Industrial Corporation. (Yefim Gordon archive)

Bottom: MiG-21bis 9483 Red of the Polskie Wojska Lotnicze. (Waclaw Holys)

TABLE OF CONTENTS

INTRODUCTION

The Mikoyan-Gurevich MiG-21, lightweight air combat fighter, is arguably the most famous military aircraft in the world. Though the Lockheed C-130 Hercules has served with more air forces, since World War II no other warplane has been manufactured in such large numbers (over 10,000 in the Soviet Union and about 2,000 in China and India), nor has any other fighter ever served with so many air forces (the current count is 56).

The MiG-21 has a fairly short range and few weapons. The first series version had just two cannons and enough ammunition for a two-second burst, while the next variant had two small missiles, but no gun. The MiG-21 was designed to climb fast to high altitudes, and excel in close combat at all altitudes. It had to be easy to maintain, tough in the harshest environments, and affordable.

This global success was the fourth in succession achieved by the MiG design bureau (*Opytno-Kon-struktorskoye Byuro* – OKB) in the immediate postwar era. This bureau had been formed in 1939 to take over the design of a small fighter with a large piston engine from Nikolai N. Polikarpov – a fighter that had proved a modest success.

In contrast to some teams, masters with piston-engine aircraft but slow to learn about jets, the MiG team took to jets like ducks to water. The inventive flair of Artyom Ivanovich Mikoyan and the erudite mathematical approach of Mikhail Iosifovich Gurevich led to the MiG-9 (NATO reporting name Fargo), MiG-15 (Fagot, which caused trouble over Korea and led to the MiG-21), MiG-17 (Fresco), and MiG-19 (Farmer), all put into series production. The MiG-21 Fishbed was the most successful of all, the name "MiG" became feared throughout the world.

MiG-21 Designations (in order of first flight)

VVS	OKB /Ye-	*Izdeliye*	ASCC
–	Ye-2	–	Faceplate
–	Ye-4	–	Fishbed
–	Ye-2A	63	Faceplate
–	Ye-5	–	Fishbed
–	Ye-50/2	–	–
MiG-21F	Ye-6T	72	Fishbed-B
MiG-21F-13	Ye-6	74	Fishbed-B
MiG-21PF	Ye-7	76	Fishbed-D
MiG-21U	Ye-6U	66	Mongol
–	Ye-8/1	–	–
MiG-21PFM	Ye-7	94	–
MiG-21R	–	94R	Fishbed-N
MiG-21S	Ye-7S	95	Fishbed-H
MiG-21PD	–	23-31	Fishbed-G
MiG-21SM	–	15	Fishbed-H
MiG-21M	–	96	Fishbed-J (1)
MiG-21I	–	21-31	– (2)
MiG-21US	–	68	Mongol-B
MiG-21MF	–	96F	Fishbed-J (3)
MiG-21SMT	–	50	Fishbed-K'
MiG-21bis	Ye-7bis	75	Fishbed-L (4) Fishbed-N
MiG-21UM	–	69	Mongol-B
MiG-21I	–	21-93	–

Notes:
1. Built by HAL in India.
2. Analog (non-digitally designed) wing testbed, /1 and /2.
3. MiG-21MT was the *Izdeliye* 96T.
4. Product numbers for MiG-21bis sub-variants are as follows:
   75A bis Lazur. Later used to denote MiG-21bis for WarPac.
   75B bis SAU. Later used for other exports.
   75P production of VVS.

Korea proved that the dogfights of 1916 and 1940 were alive and well in the 1950s. The MiG-15's combat debut in the Korean War not only set Western pulses racing, but brought about the concept of a lightweight fighter for the USSR. This was to take shape as the MiG-21.

THE CONCEPT 1

On 25 June 1950, North Korea invaded South Korea. United Nations (UN) forces sprang to their defense, so, instead of being a virtual walkover, the war lasted three years and ended in an unsatisfactory stalemate and armistice. In the course of this bitter conflict, numerous combats took place between the Soviet Union's MiG-15 and the U.S. North American F-86 Sabre. These two aircraft, the first swept-wing jet fighters to enter service, were very evenly matched. During this campaign, fighter designers all over the world studied the results. Several even visited Korea (some Americans to the South, a few Russians to the North) to talk to the pilots. The universal plea was for increased performance.

Jet propulsion had made supersonic speed possible, and supersonic aircraft traveled in almost straight lines. When they try to turn, the turn radius could be several miles. Thus, it was argued there would be no possibility of close combat, only for a single pass with cannon or a standoff missile kill. Korea proved that the dogfight was alive and well. The immediate task was to design fighters to take off quicker, climb faster, fly faster (certainly at over Mach 1.5) and higher than their opponents, and then maneuver better to quickly get into gun firing positions. The same capability was expected for a kill with a guided missile when such things became available. In turn, this meant that the aircraft had to be quite small and powered by a turbojet with afterburner for the greatest possible thrust.

Best known of the American solutions was the Lockheed F-104 Starfighter. Powered by the outstanding General Electric J79 engine, it had unrivalled straight-line performance; however, in their desire for this goal the Lockheed team made the wing incredibly small. The turning circle was enormous, and it was an unforgiving aircraft requiring experienced pilots. In France, Dassault created the Mirage III after study of Britain's Fairey Delta. This had a delta wing with an area of 35.0 m^2 (377 ft^2) and no horizontal tail; it was far from agile. The pilots were trained to slam into afterburner, point at the enemy, and fire – even when armed with a single unreliable missile. By 1957, Britain – a leader in fighter design in 1945 – had created in the Saunders-Roe SR.177, probably the best answer of all. By combining an afterburning turbojet with a fully controllable rocket in an agile airframe with adequate wing area, this aircraft promised a combination of unrivalled performance and agility

The North American F-86 Sabre proved a capable counter to the MiG-15 in the skies over Korea, but it was no pushover. Both types went on to achieve long records of service. F-86F-26-NH of 1952 illustrated. (Jay Miller collection)

The F-104 Starfighter saw comparatively little service with the "parent" air arm, being a much greater success in the export market as a multi-purpose fighter. USAF F-104A-5-LO 56-739 is one of 153 built. (Jay Miller collection)

up to over 21,000 m (70,000 ft). Unbelievably, the official view in Britain was that ground-based missiles had made all fighters obsolete. Accordingly, the SR.177 was cancelled; the English Electric Lightning was allowed to continue because "unfortunately it has proceeded too far to cancel."

In Moscow many of the Soviet Union's designers met to discuss the British belief. The collective opinion was universal: the British had gone insane. Mikoyan, delighted at the cancellation of the SR.177, was not a man to rest on his laurels. He had won with the MiG-15 partly by being good but also by being remarkably quick in design and development. The earlier rivals, Lavochkin and Yakovlev, produced many designs, but never came anywhere near competing with the MiG-15 and MiG-17. From 1952, Mikoyan's SM series contin-

ued the bureau's dominance, leading to the outstanding MiG-19. Such repeated success enabled the MiG OKB to expand, hiring not only many young graduates but also numerous experienced engineers from the Sukhoi team.

In autumn 1953, the Kremlin issued its requirement for a new fighter. The MiG OKB already had a large number of experimental prototypes using various engines. Thus, the MiG project design staff was well placed to meet the new demand for a lightweight fighter for *Frontovaya Aviatsionnaya* (Frontal Aviation), the arm of the VVS (Russian Air Force) tasked with providing tactical air power.

The Kremlin demand called for a level speed of Mach 2 at an altitude of 20 km (65,600 ft) while carrying guns. It also called for a simple radar-ranging sight with the ability later to carry air-to-air

missiles (AAMs). Each case called for operating under close ground control by the "Markham" radio network. The requirement for an agile light fighter enjoyed high priority; the fighter OKBs of Lavochkin, Mikoyan, Sukhoi, and Yakovlev carried out studies. The Central Aerodynamic and Hydrodynamic Institute (TSAGI, often rendered in English phonetically as TsAGI) tested models in transonic and supersonic tunnels to establish the best configuration. Though some work was done on models with "straight" or sharply tapered wings, forward-swept wings, and tail-less deltas, most effort was applied to mid-wing shapes with either a sharply swept or delta wing with a conventional horizontal tail. Choice of engine was clearly crucial, and the decision was made to use the Mikulin KB AM-9B.

WING CONFIGURATION 2

Official portrait of Ye-2, the first of all the prototypes that led to the MiG-21. It is parked on the snow at LII-VVS Zhukovskii, where nearly all the prototype photographs were taken, probably just before G. K. Mosolov flew it for the first time on 14 February 1955. (RSK MiG)

The MiG OKB had a reputation for rapid development. In 1954 it was put to its greatest test. It needed a variety of prototypes – with different engines – before anything could be committed to series production. Throughout, TsAGI provided aerodynamic support though the OKB was becoming more capable with high-speed wind tunnels and a new research laboratory.

The immediate objective was to follow TsAGI's principal tunnel-tested wing shapes. One was a tapered swept-wing with a sweep angle at 25% chord of 55° (the same as the MiG-19), and the other a pure delta with a leading-edge angle of 57°, which was a new shape for the OKB – and, indeed, for the USSR. Later in the 1950s, with larger prototypes, the OKB was to fly wings with different angles, but these two figures were adopted in every subsequent light-weight prototype and every MiG-21 variant.

The second objective was to hustle the engine KB of A A Mikulin into making available the new AM-11. This had been designed specifically for future light supersonic fighters by a team under Sergei K. Tumanskiy, who had joined the Mikulin KB in 1949. Following his takeover, the "AM" engine designations were replaced with a plain "R" for *reaktivnyi* (jet), or "RD" adding *dvigatel* (engine). Engines of his design were to be made in greater numbers than any other, and were a key factor in development of the MiG-21.

The AM-11 was precisely what the MiG designers wanted. A study was made of the Ye-1 (*Yedinitsa*, "single unit" – or "one off") with the AM-11. On paper a simple installation and the larger jet pipe promised to give an aerodynamically superior rear fuselage. A further study was

The snow has melted to reveal Zhukovskii's apron of large concrete squares. Note the conical inlet centre-body (first in the OKB), Mosolov looking through the integral thick windscreen, and the tailplane anti-flutter weights. (RSK MiG)

In this view the Ye-2's different skin materials stand out, as do the white borders to the national military insignia and the large sloping ventral strakes at the tail. (RSK MiG)

Large fences, extra instrumentation sensors on the nose and a cooling inlet at the fixed root of the tailplane characterize the Ye-2A, the second prototype to be powered by an AM-11. (RSK MiG)

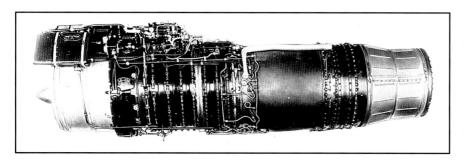

An early AM-5 single-shaft turbojet, from which stemmed all the 25,000 engines used in MiG-21s. (Yefim Gordon archive)

made in 1954 of the Ye-1 with the AM-9Ye engine plus a liquid-propellant rocket – this was designated Ye-50. While waiting for the AM-11, the MiG designers had to use an AM-9B, the simple single-shaft afterburning engine with a maximum (reheat) rating of 3,250 kg (7,165 lbs), as in the MiG-19. With this interim engine the Ye-1 became designated the Ye-2.

Compared with the AM-11 installation, the smaller engine nozzle tapered the rear fuselage, especially around the upper half. Otherwise, the Ye-2 was changed little from the stillborn Ye-1, the principal modifications being to add two-part slats on each outer wing and two quite large curved aerodynamic strakes mounted obliquely under the rear fuselage. In parallel, the MiG OKB drew the Ye-2A with the eventual AM-11 engine, and two virtually identical delta wing aircraft, the Ye-4 with the AM-9B and the Ye-5 with the

AM-11. These four types were all planned with a circular nose inlet with a small conical center-body, one-piece "slab" horizontal tails, and a unique pilot-escape system comprising an ejection seat pivoted to the rear of a one-piece transparent canopy which, upon ejection, would temporarily enclose the pilot and act as a protective windbreak.

Construction was immediately authorized for all five aircraft (these four plus the Ye-50), the Ye-2 being slightly ahead of the others. This wing was reminiscent of a MiG-19 wing, but scaled from 9.0 to 8.109 m (26 ft 7 in) span and fitted with automatic slats. The aerofoil section was the same TsAGI high-speed profile, thickness/chord ratio 6%, and it was mounted fractionally below center, with an anhedral of -3°. The root rib was extended as a fairing ahead of the leading edge and behind the trailing edge. It was carried on strong fuselage frames to avoid the need for the spars across the engine ducts.

Fuselage cross-section was almost circular, determined by the need to run the engine ducts on each side of the cockpit. The nose inlet was sharp edged and had a fixed geometry. The center-body mounted on the vertical splitter that bifurcated the ducts past the cockpit. Frame No. 26 carried a plate-type ventral airbrake, two further airbrakes being hinged under the fuselage level with the leading edge. Four fuel tanks were installed around the duct and engine, separated by firewalls with flame traps, and with non-return valves in the piping. At frame No. 28, the rear fuselage – made integral with the fin – could be detached for engine access or removal. Underneath it were two strakes, called keels, incorporating bumpers to scrape a runway without damage. In the base of the forward fuselage were two NR-30 cannons. The guns were staggered, the right hand being further forward, each fed by a 60-round belt between the engine duct and the skin.

The slab tail-planes were mounted high on the rear fuselage, on the ends of short fixed root sections,

Rearward aspect view of the Ye-2A. The port wing fence is just discernible. (RSK MiG)

The Ye-2A seen from above and behind, this time showing off the wing fences to advantage. (RSK MiG)

small blister on each side for the compass magnetometer. The rudder was operated manually, and push/pull rods in the fuselage spine operated the tail controls.

The gunsight was the ASP-5N (ASP = automatic aeroplane sight), with SRD-1 radar ranging (SRD = aeroplane range measure). The communications radio was the usual RSIU-4 VHF, with a back-sloping blade antenna behind the canopy. Other equipment included the ARK-5 radio compass (the antenna under the nose, the goniometer in the fin), *Uzel* (Knot) beacon-homing receiver, *Barii*-M (Barium) identification friend or foe (IFF), and *Sirena*-2 (Siren) radar warning receiver (RWR) system with the aft-facing antenna at the top of the fin. The AKS-5 combat cine camera was in the upper leading edge of the inlet duct splitter. Space was provided for an MRP-

1955 onto a ramp thickly populated by MiG experimental prototypes, but it was noticeably smaller than the others. Its empty weight was close to estimate at 3,687 kg (8,128 lbs), the gross weight for first flight being 5,334 kg (11,759 lbs). It was first flown by Georgii K. Mosolov on 14 February 1955. Even though it was underpowered he deemed it excellent. Performance limits were later established at 1,920 km/h (1,193 mph, about Mach 1.8) and ceiling of 19 km (62,335 ft).

Two days later Fyodor I. Burtsev flew the larger I-1. It was essentially a MiG-19 powered by a single VK-7 centrifugal-compressor turbojet. The next small prototype to fly was the Ye-4. It was partly the enthusiasm of the OKB's Pyotr Krasil'shchikov, backed up by the results of tunnel tests at TsAGI, that prompted the construction of two airframes generally similar to the Ye-2 but with the completely different delta wing. Unlike most deltas, this wing was a perfect triangle with pointed tips, dubbed *balalaika*. It differed from the Ye-2 wing in almost all respects. There was a single main spar at one-third chord running from root to tip, joined by transverse spars behind. The flaps were tracked slotted (almost Fowler) type, but rectangular. The ailerons were one-piece and quite sharply tapered. The wing contained no fuel, though it was intended that later delta wings would have portions of structure sealed to form integral tanks. At the root, the fuselage attachment rib was not extended beyond the chord of the wing.

This wing demanded a different mounting for the main landing gear. The legs had to pivot at the junction of the main and forward transverse spars, increasing the wheelbase from 4.41 to 4.48 m (14 ft 5-1/2 in to 14 ft 7 in) and track from 2.679 to 2.692 m (8 ft 7 in to 8 ft 8-1/2 in). The main legs retracted diagonally forwards, but an increase in tire size to 660 x 200

Probably taken in the 1970s, the Ye-2A served as an instructional airframe at Kharkov Aviation Institute. Various parts have been cut open to show structure and systems. (RSK MiG)

with -4° anhedral, the span being 3.726 m (12 ft 2-5/8 in), leading edge angle 55°, the broad tips parallel to the longitudinal axis. Each was driven by a single power unit at the base of the fin that had a leading-edge angle of 61°, and a

48P marker receiver for the instrument landing system.

The Ye-2 was made almost entirely of aluminum alloy, with a flush-riveted exterior. It was unpainted, except for white-bordered red stars. It emerged in early

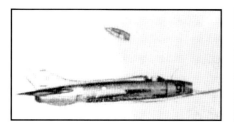

A canopy jettison is tested from one of the small number of production "MiG-23" aircraft. The pilot, probably from LII, flew back to Zhukovskii with the cockpit open. (Yefim Gordon archive)

This Ye-2A was snapped by a McGraw-Hill camera at the 1956 Tushino air display. All the West knew was that it was called Faceplate by NATO. (Yefim Gordon archive)

The Ye-4 was so smooth it looked like a plastic model. Note the large underwing fence, and the "gear extended" indicator rod above the wing. The AM-9 engine resulted in a long rear fuselage tapered mainly from above. The ventral strakes differed slightly from those of the Ye-2. (RSK MiG)

mm (25-3/4 in x 7-3/4 in) made the retracted wheel create small blisters above and below the wing root.

The six fuselage tanks were restricted to 1,300 kg (about 1,625 liters, 357 gallons). The rudder was made slightly smaller by extending the height of the fixed portion at its base, above the jet pipe. The rest of the aircraft was almost identical to the Ye-2, except the improved SRD-3M *Konus* (Cone) ranging radar in the inlet center-body. The Ye-4 was first flown by Grigoriy A. Sedov on 16 June 1955. OKB testing continued until 20 September 1956, principally in an effort to improve performance. Contrary to prediction, level speed was only 1,296 km/h (805 mph, about Mach 1.21) and service ceiling 16,400 m (53,800 ft). These distressing results were puzzling, and time was short.

Mikoyan drove his team to find solutions quickly; modifications centered upon the wing. First, two large under fences were added but later replaced by three shallower

fences on the upper surface. Next, the detachable tips were removed, reducing span to 7.149 m (23 ft 5-1/2 in). Finally, the chord of the outer leading edge was extended, ending at a sharp "dogtooth" at its inboard end to create a powerful vortex at high angle of attack (AoA). The Ye-4 was handed to the LII-MAP (Ministry of Aviation Industry Flight Research Institute) for high-AoA research, repeatedly holding an angle of 25°. The OKB re-engined this aircraft, first with the AM-9D (RD-9D) and then the RD-9I, both slightly more powerful than the original AM-9B. With the latest standard of wing and RD-9I, Sedov flew the Ye-4 on 5 September 1956.

In September 1955, rival Sukhoi flew the S-1, first of a series of larger experimental prototypes with swept and delta wings. Mikoyan was deeply concerned to hear that the S-1 immediately hit 2,000 km/h (1,242 mph). This posed big problems for the MiG OKB. Despite

every effort, little more could really be done. Then, on 9 January 1956, two new MiG prototypes made their maiden flights on the same day. These were the Ye-5 and Ye-50-1.

In fact, by late 1955 the MAP was certain that one of the MiG light fighters would enter production so it allocated the series designations MiG-21 to the delta and "MiG-23" (Type 63) to the swept-wing version. It expected the MiG-21 to be built by Aviation Factory No. 31 at Tbilisi and the MiG-23 to be produced by Plant 21 at Gorkiy. At this time, both the Ye-2 and the rival S-1 had so out-performed the troubled Ye-4 delta that the general consensus was that the MiG-23 would probably be chosen. The first order placed on the Gorkiy plant was for five MiG-23 pre-series prototypes to the latest Ye-2A swept-wing standard. (Of course, later the designation MiG-23 was re-used for a totally different aircraft, the "Flogger.")

The first remarkably simple, AM-11 engine was installed on the third delta airframe, the waiting Ye-5. This aircraft flew on 9 January 1956, in the hands of Vladimir A. Nefyedov. The wing was similar to that of the second Ye-4 with three upper-surface fences, but with the pointed tips in place. The fuselage was unchanged, except for a startling redesign of the aft air brake that took the form of a bulged panel of irregular outline with four large holes. The removable rear fuselage was shorter and less

The Ye-4 had a wing of pure delta (triangular) form, with a leading-edge angle of 57°, main wheel blisters and "slab" tailplanes with fixed roots. (RSK MiG)

The official photographs of the Ye-4 were taken with G. A. Sedov in the cockpit, who obviously had an excellent all-round view. The delta configuration left inadequate room for a Red Star on the fuselage. (RSK MiG)

The Ye-4 delta from behind. Compare with the similar angle on the Ye-2A. Engine is the RD-9I. (RSK MiG)

View of the Ye-4 showing the 57° sweep "perfect" delta wing. (RSK MiG)

tapered. The fixed portion at the root of each tailplane was extended forward to start at a ram inlet to provide engine bay cooling, and tailplane span was increased. This transformed performance, level speed at optimum height was established at 1,970 km/h (1,224 mph, about Mach 1.85), service ceiling was found to be 17,650 m (57,900 ft), and a height of 5 km (3.1 miles) could be reached 1.6 minutes from brake release.

However, all was not well with the new engine. There was a severe fire in the engine bay on 20 February 1956. Eight flights were completed between 26 March and 19 May, before there was a catastrophic turbine failure. All RD-11 engines were grounded in October 1956. Though the Ye-5 could easily have used up all the RD-11 engines available, the first were earmarked for the two improved swept-wing Ye-2As. The first of these flew in the hands of Sedov on 17 February 1956. These aircraft combined the forward fuselage of a Ye-2 with the rear of a Ye-5 and an improved Ye-2 wing, without slats, but with an enormous fence across the upper surface. The slats of the Ye-2 had been found to open asymmetrically with, for instance, any significant degree of sideslip. In simulated combat this could throw the pilot off his aim by imparting sudden disturbances in pitch and roll. The fences improved the effectiveness of the ailerons, especially at high AoA.

Ye-2A/3, the first pre-production MiG-23 (Type 63), was handed to LII MAP Center at Zhukovskiy. Here A. P. Bogorodskii carried out a series

Another Ye-4 modification was to add a narrow sharp strip along the trailing edge of the rudder. This was repeated on later aircraft. (RSK MiG)

The single Ye-4 was later modified with slightly clipped wing tips and three fences on each side above the wing. The engine was replaced by an RD-9I. (RSK MiG)

Powered by an AM-11, the Ye-5 had a fuselage almost identical to that of the Ye-2A. (RSK MiG)

The Ye-5 had an upward-sloping PVD boom, and a cooling inlet ahead of each fixed tailplane root. (RSK MiG)

of dead-stick (gliding) landings, without problems. Another MiG-23, bearing callsign "9I," was painted with camera index markings and used as an LL (flying laboratory) to help develop the crew-escape system. However, it was the Ye-5 that was chosen for development.

On 24 June 1956, examples of both the Ye-2A and Ye-4/-5 flew low over Moscow Tushino airfield in the annual Aviation Day parade. The resultant pictures taken by Western observers present were of poor quality. The NATO Allied Standards Coordinating Committee, which invented names for all Soviet military aircraft, called the swept-wing versions "Faceplate" and the deltas "Fishbed." For years afterwards NATO believed that the former was selected for production.

MAP planned in 1957 to build 10 pre-production MiG-21s based on the Ye-5 at Tbilisi and six MiG-23s based on the Ye-2A at Gorkiy. By the end of 1956 both Ye-5 prototypes had flown, and Plant No. 31 at Tbilisi had built five pre-series RD-11 powered MiG-21 aircraft for further testing. Intensive testing showed that the deltas had greater internal fuel capacity, a higher rate of roll, generally better turn radius, lighter structure, and marginally better supersonic performance than rivals with swept wings. Apart from range and combat radius, which was basically an engine problem, the Ye-5s met all predicted performance figures. The Ye-5/2 was later used for ski tests.

CONFIGURATION

Official side view of the Ye-50-1, with LII-MAP pilot V. G. Mukhin in the cockpit. The PVD boom was inclined downwards, and a long pipe fairing preceded each tailplane. (RSK MiG)

By the end of 1956 the MiG OKB had a clear idea how it would proceed in developing the delta wing MiG-21. In parallel, it continued to work on a mixed-power (turbojet-plus-rocket) interceptor. This was the Ye-50, already mentioned.

In 1946–'48 the OKB had designed and flown two prototypes of Aircraft J (I-270), a short-range interceptor powered solely by a twin-chamber rocket engine. Now, in parallel with the light fighter program, it was gaining extensive experience testing larger supersonic fighters with booster rockets added underneath, but had not flown a true mixed-power aircraft with a pilot-controllable rocket engine permanently installed. The Ye-50 airframe was based on that of the Ye-2A. The main differences concerned the fuel tanks and the aft fuselage behind Frame No. 28A, which was completely new. The main engine was the AM-9Ye, by 1956 called the RD-9Ye, fed from a group of kerosene tanks in the modified tank bays in the center fuselage.

The Ye-50-1 reveals its superimposed engines, as well as the outwards-inclined leg doors that were to be a feature of all MiG-21s. (RSK MiG)

Eventually the OKB received funding for three Ye-50 aircraft, each to be assigned to a pilot from Zhukovskiy. The Ye-50-1 was completed in late 1955 with normal instruments and electronics for flight-testing, but without military equipment. The pilot assigned to it was Valentin G. Mukhin from the LII-MAP. Using the turbojet alone, he opened the flight test program on 9 January 1956. The first rocket engine flight was on 8 June 1956, when it was operated for 11 seconds at an altitude of 9 km (5.6 miles). Unfortunately, at the conclusion of the 18th flight on 14 July, the Ye-50-1 made a hard landing and was damaged beyond repair.

A view showing the Ye-50-1's spine inlet for the rocket bay and the vent on the fin below the Red Star. Also note the single shallow ventral strake under a long pipe fairing. (RSK MiG)

The Ye-50-2 differed in having the lower portion of the rudder transferred to the fin below its base; at the same time, a sharp-edged strip was added at the rudder's trailing edge to increase chord. This aircraft was fully equipped as a fighter, with two NR-30 guns, Grad (Hail) radar ranging sight, and Barii-M IFF. The pilot assigned was Valentin P. Vasin,

Forward view of the Ye-50-1. The sloping PVD boom is clearly visible. (RSK MiG)

Two photographs showing the Ye-50-2 taking off from Zhukovskii with both engines in operation. In the darker view steam from decomposing peroxide is pouring from the fin vent. (Yefim Gordon archive)

Cine film still showing the Ye-50-2 at Mikoyan's OKB-155 with the S-155 motor opened up for attention. This aircraft is believed to have been painted dark grey. (Yefim Gordon archive)

also from the LII-MAP. The loaded weight had risen to above 8,500 kg (18,739 lbs). This made takeoffs, using only the low-powered turbojet, require almost the entire Zhukovskiy runway. Also, the very limited kerosene capacity limited range to below 450 km (280 miles).

The third aircraft, the Ye-50-3, had a redesigned nose section. The new nose incorporated a more efficient conical center-body of Oswatitsch double-shock type, focusing two oblique shocks and one normal shock on the sharp peripheral lip. This gave improved pressure recovery at high supersonic Mach numbers. The cone was arranged to translate (move axially) for best efficiency. It slid in and out according to Mach number, and the control system required a small fairing above the nose. This principle was to be a feature of all production MiG-21s. The pilot assigned to this aircraft was N. A. Korovin, from the NII-VVS. On one of his first flights in autumn 1957, the S-155 malfunctioned catastrophically. Korovin had to eject, but was tragically killed. To avoid future incidents OKB-155 developed the SK-3 (KM-1) ejection seat.

The Ye-50 performed well, and the mixed-power formula seemed suitable for a superior high-altitude interceptor. In 1956, before the Ye-50-3 had flown, the MiG OKB had proposed various improved versions. Most of them were based on the airframe of the Ye-2A/Ye-5 with

the RD-11 engine. This fuselage was considerably shorter than that of any of the Ye-50s, and drastic action was needed to accommodate the required quantity of kerosene and rocket propellants. The obvious answer was to scab on an additional ventral tank.

From the start the MiG lightweight prototypes were well matched to the Area Rule, because the wing volume was small. Gorkiy was contracted to build a single prototype designated Ye-50A. It was expected that this aircraft, in a refined form, would go into production as the MiG-23U. The U did not signify *Uchyebniy* (trainer), but *Uskoritel'*, which literally translates to accelerated. The OKB designation was Type 64. After prolonged testing with several other MiG prototypes (including service experience with the SM-51 and SM-52) and the Yak-27V, and planned tests with a mixed-power Sukhoi T-43, it was decided at Minister level that rocket engines were not the way to go. The Dushkin KB was promptly closed, leaving the Ye-50A program in limbo and the prototype incomplete.

This left the light-fighter program powered by an afterburning turbojet, which Mikoyan welcomed. By 1957, as a result of intensive testing of the experimental Type 37F turbojets, Tumanskiy could offer an improved engine, the RD-11F-300. This engine retained a similar gas generator (compressor,

combustion chamber and turbine), but featured an improved afterburner, enabling maximum dry and reheat ratings to be established at 3,880 and 5,740 kg (8,554 and 12,654 lbs), respectively. This was available for the next group of three light delta prototypes constructed in 1957–'58, designated Ye-6. These were regarded as pre-production aircraft, built under chief engineer I. I. Rotchik, assisted by the Minayev's systems laboratory.

The first of this family, the Ye-6/1, had a wing based upon that of the

The Ye-50-3 had a longer nose, modified tail, revised rocket installation, and no ventral radio antenna. (RSK MiG)

Overhead view of the Ye-50-3, showing that the fairings ahead of the tailplane roots were also aerodynamic strakes. The Ye-50s had no main wheel blisters. (RSK MiG)

Ye-5, with the tips removed, the span reduced to 7.154 m (23 ft 5-5/8 in). Wing chord increased at the rear, the ailerons reduced in span and each wing fitted with a hardpoint. The tail end of the fuselage was considerably enlarged in both diameter and length, improving aerodynamics. The horizontal tail was moved to the rear, reaching beyond the new nozzle and also moved down to the mid-level, mounted horizontally, so that each tip stayed in the original place. The tailplane was enlarged to retain the span at 3.74 m (12 ft 2 in), but the fixed portion at the root was almost eliminated. The vertical tail area was slightly increased and the fin was joined to the spine by a dorsal fin incorporating the q-feel ram inlet. The curved diagonal ventral strakes were replaced by a single large ventral fin on the centerline. A circular braking parachute was housed above this a bay in the left side of the fuselage. It was connected by cable to an anchor under fin.

The nose inlet was redesigned; the sharp outer lip was inclined slightly to improve pressure recovery at high AoA. The conical centerbody was arranged to translate to three positions. The canopy was a refined version of that tested on the Ye-2A/6. To prevent a repetition of the failure that killed Korovin, the rearmost arched frame was made even stronger. It had two blister fairings over the seat thrust pivots,

and the fixed rear frame was strengthened. In turn, the lower tailplanes required the front airbrakes to be moved forward and changed in shape. Finally, almost all the equipment carried was production, not experimental.

The Ye-6/1 was ready for factory testing in May 1958, and in the same month the Ye-4 and Ye-5 prototypes finished comprehensive tests to establish the optimum aerodynamics of supersonic delta-wing fighters. The Ye-4 had flown over 100 times up to Mach 1.45, including spinning. In a further 98 flights, the Ye-5 had progressed to Mach 1.85 at 18 km (59.055 ft). The various Ye-2 and Ye-2A prototypes added a further 250 flights.

Flights of the Ye-6 family opened on 20 May 1958, when Ye-6/1 was flown by Nefyodov from LII-MAP Zhukovskiy. It proved to be an excellent aircraft, immediately establishing a level Mach number of 2.05 at 12,050 m (39,500 ft), equivalent to about 2,181 km/h (1,355 mph). On the seventh flight on 28 May, the engine suffered a flameout at about 18 km (11.2 miles) high. Nefyedov tried to restart and failed. He was eventually commanded by radio to eject, but determined to save the aircraft and its valuable instrumentation record, continued trying to restart the engine as he neared Zhukovskiy. The emergency electric pump was eventually switched in, but too late to prevent total loss of

The Ye-50-3 was painted pale grey overall. Like the Ye-2 family, the ailerons were in two sections – inner and outer. (RSK MiG)

control on final approach. The Ye-6/1 crashed inverted, its pilot dying in the hospital of severe burns.

This was a great blow to the LII and to the whole MiG OKB. By this time the Ye-6/2 "22" was almost complete. Rostislav A. Belyakov – then deputy chief designer and since 1971 General Director of the Mikoyan bureau – forcefully proposed removing the electric standby pump and installing duplicate hydraulics throughout, and Mikoyan accepted this. The Ye-6/2 was extensively reworked and finally flown by Konstantin K. Kokkinaki on 15 September 1958 with a fully redundant hydraulic system. After completing 15 test flights at Zhukovskiy the Ye-6/2 was relocated at Krasnovodsk, on the Caspian

A photograph of the Ye-50-3 at high altitude with the S-155 at full power. Note the duplicate RSIU-4V VHF antenna under the fuselage. (Yefim Gordon archive)

Artist's impression of the unbuilt Ye-50A, produced by retouching a familiar picture of the Ye-2. (Yefim Gordon archive)

shore opposite Baku, to avoid the severe winter. Altogether the Ye-6/2 made 46 flights, having only three engine changes.

The Ye-6/2 introduced a cleaner wing. The three fences were all removed, replaced by a single very small fence in the same location as the outermost of the original three. On each side of the nose a rectangular auxiliary air inlet was added, to help prevent compressor stalls. Operative NR-30 guns were installed, with the magazine capacity reduced to 30 rounds each.

The third aircraft, the Ye-6/3, "23," made its first flight in December 1958, and was also based at Krasnovodsk. This aircraft

introduced a pair of auxiliary engine air-inlets, in this case almost square and located immediately below the tapered front end of the wing root rib. It was also the first of the family to have yaw vanes on the PVD, and the first to be fitted with the SRO-2 (*Khrom*, "chromium," family) IFF transponder, with antennae beside the nose leg and on top of the fin.

The Ye-6/3 was also the first to test the centerline tank, mounted on a single shallow pylon. This tank extended the range at high altitude from about 1,400 to 1,800 km (870 to 1,118 miles). The Ye-6/2 and /3 completed OKB testing in 61 flights. At the conclusion, Kokkinaki

reported that a series MiG-21 could be "flown by any normal pilot, not only by special men." The recommended never exceed Mach number was set at 2.05. In every flight regime and configuration the stability, control, and all-round maneuverability were judged excellent. Accordingly, the Council of Ministers decided to put the aircraft into series production at two factories, No. 21 at Gorkiy for the VVS and, for export customers, at MMZ Znamya Truda (Banner of Labor), the former factory No. 30, in Moscow.

While the Ye-6/2 and /3 were beginning their flight test programs in the fourth quarter of 1958 a copy of the American AIM-9 Sidewinder

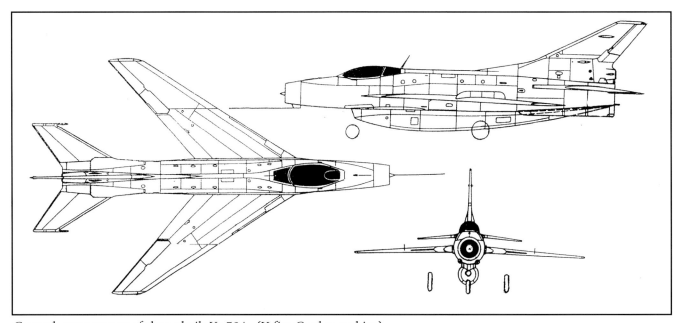

General arrangement of the unbuilt Ye-50A. (Yefim Gordon archive)

Apart from the three fences on each wing and the telemetry antenna behind the nose landing gear, the Ye-6/1 looked almost identical to the first series MiG-21. The pilot is almost certainly V. A. Nefyedov. Note the slightly sloping lip round the nose inlet, and the large central under-fin. (RSK MiG)

K. K. Kokkinaki's Ye-6/2 was later modified with a unique wing with a kinked leading edge to give a tip broad enough to carry APU-13 rail launchers for K-13 missiles. (RSK MiG)

Red 22, the modified Ye-6/2, seen head-on with K-13 missiles on the wing tips and centerline air brake open. (RSK MiG)

Looking down on the Ye-6/3 (Red 23) prototype of the MiG-21F. Nothing projects above the wing but a small fence outboard and the flap actuator fairing. (RSK MiG)

air-to-air missile was being developed. In September 1958, many Sidewinders had failed to detonate when fired by Nationalist aircraft from Taiwan against Chinese fighters. One was passed to the Soviet Union, where OKB-134 did a remarkably fast "Chinese copy." This was the K-13, service designation R-3S, with passive infrared homing. The launch weight was 73.5kg (162lb, rather heavier than the American original). On 11 February 1959 the MiG bureau made the first missile test flight.

The obvious carrier was the MiG-21, and in 1960 the Ye-6/2 was returned to Factory No. 155 to be modified. After preliminary model tests it was decided to fit new wings, carrying the missiles on the tips. These were unchanged inboard of the rib separating the flap and aileron. The outer section had the leading-edge sweep reduced to 48°, giving a tip chord large enough for an APU-13 rail launcher. No fence was required. It was expected that the change would enhance agility, but during aircraft flight tests followed by live firings from September 1960 to April 1961, the results were unpredictable and generally unsatisfactory. Accordingly, it was decided to fire this missile from APU-13 launchers mounted under the wings. The Ye-6/2 was the only aircraft of the MiG-21 family to have this basic change in wing shape.

After the completion of its OKB testing, the Ye-6/3 was fitted with an up-rated RD-11 engine and set two world records. On 31 October 1959, Mosolov set a straight-line record for absolute speed over a 15/25 km (9.3/15.5 miles) course at 2,388 km/h (1,483 mph), one run being at 2,504 km/h (1,556 mph, about Mach 2.356). The record was submitted to the Fédération Aéronautique Internationale (FAI) with the fictitious aircraft designation "Ye-66." A second record was set on 16 September 1960 by Kokkinaki, for speed round a 100-km closed circuit, the average being 2,148.66 km/h (1,334 mph), with a peak ground speed of 2,499 km/h (1,552 mph).

It is worth concluding this chapter by taking the reader back to the early 1960s. Western intelligence agencies were almost totally

The Ye-6/3 posed with open cockpit, three-position cone retracted, 490 liter (107.8 gallon) centerline tank, and unusual pylons carrying UB-16-57U launchers. (RSK MiG)

In this view of the Ye-6/3, it is possible to see the three-rod antennae of the SRO-2 Khrom IFF on top of the fin. (RSK MiG)

Official side view of the Ye-6/3. Behind the nosewheel leg the downward hemisphere IFF antenna can just be discerned. In the MiG-21 this was positioned further aft. (RSK MiG)

A September 1960 picture taken after the Ye-6/3 had gained two world records as the fictitious "Ye-66." Mikoyan is standing between K. K. Kokkinaki (leather jacket) and Mosolov (uniform). (RSK MiG)

ignorant of the MiG-21. In 1960 a hardback book *Warplanes of the World* appeared including a complete entry on the MiG-21, called "Face-plate," having swept wings, a weight "over 20,000 lbs," armament of "three 37mm cannons," and possibly "an auxiliary rocket motor under the rear fuselage." In another entry, the actual aircraft, called "Fishbed," was "designed by Pavel Sukhoi . . . capable of Mach 1.5 to 1.7."

Even after the real MiG-21 had appeared (in several forms) at an air-show in 1961, many experts insisted that nobody would build such small lightweight aircraft. When a photo-graph appeared of the much bigger twin-engine Mikoyan Ye-152A, this was hailed as the "real MiG-23" – the actual production aircraft. One who held out against this was Bill Gun-ston, who, in the 7 November 1963 issue of *Flight International*, described

this aircraft as "only a prototype," and its missiles as "mock-ups." This prompted a reader to send in a faked model photograph purporting to show the MiG-23 firing a missile, using cotton-wool smoke. After care-ful scrutiny by the journal's editor, who during World War II had been a senior air intelligence officer, and dis-cussion with experts in the UK Min-istry of Defense, this picture was pro-nounced "undoubtedly authentic!"

MiG-21 In Detail

There never was a production "MiG-21." The initial production fighter, built at Factory No. 21 at Gorkiy, had the service designation MiG-21F (*Forsazh*, boosted), the factory designation being Ye-6T and the Type number (or *Izdeliye* – product number) being 72. In conformity with standard practice throughout the Soviet Union, a team of engineers with intimate knowledge of the MiG-21 took up residence at the factory, partly to assist the factory and partly to feed back problems to the OKB. Three of the first series machines were retained by the OKB as Ye-6T development aircraft. Differences from the Ye-6/3 were minimal. The following describes the initial standard of build of the MiG-21F:

Structure

The airframe was designed to an ultimate load factor of 7g. Ruling material was D16-T aluminum alloy, with almost all joints being made by rivets or precision bolts, flush on the outer skin. Spar booms were high-strength V-65-1 or V-25. The skins above and below wing integral tanks were V-95 alloy, highly stressed joints 30KhGSA (*Chromansil*), or 30KhGSN2A steel, with ML5-T4 or M25-T4 at other stress concentrations, a few parts Ak-4-1, magnesium alloy, or (top of fin and front of under-fin) glass-fiber. There were no integrally stiffened machined parts, but the entire structure of the main wing box was chemically milled.

Wing

The wing was pure delta (triangle) with cropped tips, aerofoil profile TsAGI S-12s, thickness/chord

The pressurized and air-conditioned cockpit of a MiG-21F-13. The instrumentation was conventional for the time. Metal armor was installed behind seat and on the headrest, with further protection from the thick structural wall planks. The main canopy was made of blown acrylic with a bullet-proof windscreen 62 mm thick and electric heater layer. (Jay Miller collection)

MiG-21F nose section. On each side of the nose was a rectangular automatic auxiliary inlet door that opened inwards by hydraulic ram linked to inlet control system. This improved duct airflow in yawed flight and helped prevent violent compressor stalls. (Yefim Gordon archive)

MiG-21F tail section. The vertical tail had a 60° leading-edge sweep, the thickness/chord ratio was 6%, the area was 3.8 m² including the rudder with aerodynamic and mass balance carried on three hinges. Horizontal tailplanes were carried on swept hinge spigots. (Yefim Gordon archive)

ratio (root) 4.2% (tip) 5.0%, span 7154 mm (23 ft 5-5/8 in), MAC (mean aerodynamic chord) 4,002 mm, root chord 5.97 mm, area 23.0 m² (247.6 ft²), aspect ratio 2.2, leading edge sweep 57°, incidence 0°, anhedral -2°. It had one main spar, one chief transverse spar, secondary spars at leading and trailing edge of fixed part of wing, 26 ribs ahead of main spar all at 90° to leading edge, 12 ribs behind principal transverse spar parallel to longitudinal axis. Skins tapered from 2.5 mm at root to 1.5 mm at tip. Wings attached to the fuselage by forged and machined root ribs with eight root attachments picking up on five fuselage frames. Leading edge featured a fixed, small fence with a height 7% of MAC was on the upper surface 0.67 m from tip. It had rectangular TsAGI slotted flaps, each 0.935 m², were track-mounted and hydraulically extended to a maximum of 24.5° for takeoff and 44.5° for landing. It had tapered tabless ailerons, each 0.51 m², and both were aerodynamically balanced and left with mass balance. The main landing gears pivoted at junction of the main and transverse spars, folding into triangular space between them. Two tanks were integral within the wing structure. The front tank was bounded by ribs Nos. 1 through 6, with upper and lower skins of V-95 alloy. Ribs No. 13 and No. 15 ahead of main spar each were forged with a single integral boss to support a pylon for underwing loads. Each wing had 20 access hatches with screwed covers.

Fuselage

The fuselage was an area-ruled semi-monocoque with basic cross sections vertical ellipses. Maximum width was 1,242 mm (48.9 in). It was made in two sections joined just behind the fixed part of the wing at frame Nos. 28 and 28A. It had few stringers; skin thickness was 1.2 mm. A sharp-lipped circular nose with an inlet of 690 mm diameter to expanding (diffuser) circular duct contained the upper and lower narrow struts. These carried a circular-section center-body with forward portion comprising a pointed cone able to translate. This was driven automatically by a hydraulic actuator controlled by the air data system (density and absolute temperature) and also by power demand and engine RPM. The cone

The MiG-21F-13 undercarriage. Each main gear unit had a single vertical shock strut carrying KT-27 wheels, pneumatic disc brakes with anti-skid system, and 660 x 200 mm tires. The legs were retracted hydraulically diagonally forwards and inwards while the wheel remained upright. (Yefim Gordon archive)

The canopy on the MiG-21F was unique in being forward hinged. The plate above the ejection seat was compressed downward when the canopy was closed, arming the ejection seat. (Yefim Gordon archive)

fully retracted up to Mach 1.5, intermediate position from Mach 1.5 to 1.9, and fully forward (to focus shock waves on the inlet lip and reduce annular area for airflow to below 93% of maximum) at over Mach 1.9.

On each side of the nose between frames No. 3/4, a rectangular automatic auxiliary inlet door opened inwards by hydraulic ram linked to inlet control system. This improved duct airflow in yawed flight and avoided violent compressor stalls. At frame No. 6, the duct bifurcated to pass on both sides of the cockpit. The inner as well as outer walls were circular, the ducts coming together again at frame No. 22 to form a circular tube on the centerline, allowing smooth airflow to the engine. Beside frame No. 10, just below the forward tip of the wing root rib on each side, an automatic auxiliary inlet with a spring-loaded suck-in door provided additional airflow under conditions of high power demand and low ram pressure (e.g., on takeoff). Between frame Nos. 3 and 6, the radio and equipment bay sat above, and the nose landing gear bay sat below. The pressurized cockpit was between frames Nos. 6 and 11. The fuel tanks sat between frame Nos. 11 and 28. The forward air brakes hinged to frame No. 11; each were 0.38 m² and driven hydraulically to

25°. The guns (later, right-hand only) were at the lower level between frames Nos. 11 and 16. Steel reinforcing skin was installed ahead of the muzzles. The main landing gear wheel bay was outboard of the (by now circular) engine air duct between frame Nos. 16 and 20. The drop tank pylon was between frame Nos. 16 and 22; aft air brake 0.47m² was hinged to frame No. 25 and driven hydraulically to 40°. The rear section had a total of 111 screwed or hinged service openings.

Tail

The tail section of the fuselage had 13 frames, and was detachable at frame No. 28A. The engine bay extended from frame Nos. 29 and 34, incorporating parts of high-carbon steel. The parabrake (braking parachute) box was on the lower left side beside ventral fin, extending over almost the entire length of section with maximum depth 352 mm. The forward portion of the radio-transparent glass-fiber served as a telemetry antenna. The vertical tail had a 60° leading-edge sweep, the skin was 0.4 mm (fin) 0.8 mm (rudder), the profile was S-11 symmetric, the thickness/chord ratio was 6%, the area was 3.8 m² including the 0.965 m² rudder with aerodynamic and mass balance carried

on three hinges. Horizontal (anhedral now 0°) tailplanes were carried on swept hinge spigots. The thickness/chord ratio was 6%, leading edge sweep was 55°, area (total) was 3.94m², span (including tip anti-flutter masses) was 3.74m.

Powerplant

The engine was a Tumanskiy RD-11F-300, Type 37F, two-shaft turbojet with afterburner. It had a maximum dry rating of 3,880 kg (8,554 lbs), with maximum afterburner of 5,740kg (12,654 lbs). It featured an LP spool with three stages of axial blades driven by single-stage LP turbine with solid shrouded blades. The first compressor stage overhung ahead of the front bearing with no preceding inlet guide vanes (in mid-1950s, both innovations) and with transonic airflow over blades at full power. The HP spool had five stages of axial blades, and was driven by a single-stage HP turbine with 96 solid shrouded blades. It had no variable stators, a maximum airflow 63.7 kg (140.4 lbs) per second, and an overall pressure ratio 8.0. A can-annular combustion chamber with two chambers was modified to house high-energy discharge igniters.

The afterburner had three spray rings and a multi-flap variable nozzle. The engine used a single-button electric starting cycle and a single-

400-liter centerline drop tank. This cruciform-finned aluminum tank held 490 liters (108 gallons) but, due to the induced drag when fitted, could only be used up to speeds below Mach 1. (Yefim Gordon archive)

lever throttle. A primary fuel pump with a precise electro-mechanical regulator maintained constant RPM, the thrust being varied by fuel flow. An afterburner fuel pump was scheduled to permit augmentation light up at low flow rate to give an almost imperceptible cut-in of afterburner, thereafter rising with smooth variation of thrust to very high flow rate at takeoff. The nozzle was controlled by an electrically signaled hydraulic system with three rams driving actuation ring. The auxiliary supply of both fuel and bottled gaseous oxygen facilitated relight at extreme altitudes and low forward speeds. The main accessory gearbox under the engine was driven by an HP spool with nine drive faces: seven normally occupied by starter/generator, two hydraulic pumps, two fuel pumps, air compressor and tachometer-generator. The sixth-stage bleed air was fed to the cockpit environmental control system; the fuel tanks and tank were used for starting fuel. The weight of the equipped engine was 1,182 kg (2,606 lbs). The installed engine compressor inlet pressed against the rubber sealing ring at frame No. 22, and was supported by the upper mount at frame No. 25. The rear steady was at frame No. 28 with the afterburner being cantilevered. The engine bay was divided into six sealed fire zones.

Cockpit

The cockpit extended from frames Nos. 6 to 11. It was pressurized (maximum dP 25kPA, about 3.6 lb/in^2) and air-conditioned, with temperature kept at 15±5° C. The instrumentation was conventional for the time. The main panel was vertical and very deep. Metal armor rested behind the seat and on the headrest, providing further protection from the thick structural wall planks. There was a fixed transparent fairing downstream of canopy. The main canopy was made of blown acrylic, incorporating a multi-ply, bullet-proof windscreen 62 mm thick and electric heater layer. This was all in a single light alloy frame hinged at the front and raised to 50° by a pneumatic ram. When closed, the canopy locked by side latches, with the rear arched frame resting on lugs on each side at top of SK cartridge-fired seat. This was usable above altitude of 110 m (361 ft) and up to an indicated airspeed of 1,100 km/h. At moderate airspeeds the pilot could choose to use sequenced ejection, in which the canopy is jettisoned separately and the seat fired 0.25 seconds later. The usual procedure is to fire the seat with face-blind, the lugs taking the rear end of canopy with it. The rotation of the canopy automatically unlatched the front attachments and freed the canopy, thus providing windbreak around the pilot. The pilot's head was protected by a pivoted arm at top of seat headrest, which before each flight was preset and locked according to pilot's height.

Flying Controls

The aircraft featured a simple control and three-axis stabilization system. The lateral is controlled solely by ailerons, each driven ±20° by a BU-45 or B4-45 booster in hydraulic booster system, signaled by push/pull rods and bell cranks inside wing leading edge. There is no autopilot in the MiG-21F, but the MiG-21F-13 ailerons are linked to a single-channel KAP-2 autopilot giving control in roll only. They are disengaged by any bank angle exceeding 35°. It operated in two regimes, damping and stabilization for night or bad weather. Control in pitch was accomplished by both "stabilators" (tailplanes) driven together through angular range +7°/-16.5° by a single BU-44 power unit with two chambers – one in each hydraulic system. The output was modulated by the ARU-3V artificial-feel system served by air data sensors and a small ram inlet in the dorsal fin. Lateral and pitch trim was driven without surface tabs by rocking switch on stick.

The rudder was driven by manual rods/bell cranks up to ±25°.

Landing Gear

Three units formed the tricycle landing gear, with a track of 2,692 mm (106 in) and wheelbase of 4,806 mm (189.2 in). Each main unit single vertical shock strut carried KT-27 wheels, pneumatic disc brakes with anti-skid system, and 660 x 200 mm tires. Inflation pressure was variable from 0.78 to 1.01 MPa (maximum 148 lbs/in²). Legs were retracted hydraulically, diagonally forwards and inwards while the wheel remained upright, thus pivoting 87° relative to the leg. The legs were housed in a small bay outboard of an air duct between fuselage frames Nos. 16 and 20. A door was hinged up from below by its own hydraulic jack. Nose gear with a single vertical strut was supported on a freely castoring levered trailing fork carrying the KT-38 wheels with pneumatic anti-skid twin-shoe drum brakes and 500 x 180 mm tires (normal inflation pressure 0.58 MPa, 110 lbs/in²). They retracted hydraulically forwards into a narrow bay between frame Nos. 3 and 6 with left/right doors. The braking parachute was circular. Its area was 16 m² (172 ft²). It was housed in a heat-insulated box in the bottom of the fuselage above the left front of the ventral fin. A cable ran back to anchor at the rear end of the ventral fin.

Systems

Fuel

Fuel grades were kerosene T-1, T-2, or TS-1. MiG-21F and MiG-21F-13 (see next chapter) from series numbers 74210701 to 74210814 were provided with six flexible protected cells in the fuselage with capacities of 235/720/265/200/240/240 liters, plus two rear integral wing tanks 190/190, for a total of 2,280 liters (501.5 Imp gal). MiG-21F-13 from 74210815 was as

Underwing pylon with APU-13 rail launcher. This rail could be fitted for K-13 or improved K-13A (R-3S) infra-red homing missiles, with an effective range of from 1 to 7 km (0.62 to 4.35 miles). (Yefim Gordon)

Rocket pod for 16 spin-stabilized non-guided air-to-ground 57 mm rockets. (Yefim Gordon archive)

before but with four integral wing tanks 175/175/110/110, giving a total of 2,470 liters (543 gallons), of which 2,340 liters (515 gallons) was usable without the onset of stability problems. The centerline cruciform-finned aluminum drop tank held 490 liters (108 gallons) but was only usable up to Mach 1.

Hydraulics

Two autonomous hydraulic systems shared separate halves of one tank. They were both filled with AMG-10 mineral oil and energized by separate engine-driven NP-34M-1T pumps to 180-215 kg/cm² (max 20.59 MPa, nominal 3,000 lbs/in²),

with reservoirs at the base of the fin. The systems were designated General and Booster. The General system served the nose cone, landing gear, auxiliary inlet (anti-compressor stall) doors, air brakes, flaps, afterburner nozzle, automatic brakes (to stop wheel rotation on takeoff), one chamber of tailplane power unit, and the standby (back-up) aileron drive. The Booster system served the normal aileron actuator and the other half of the tailplane power unit. If either circuit fails, the remaining system can provide full control power.

Electric

The engine drives a GSR-ST-1200VT-2I rotary machine able to function as both a DC generator and as a main engine starter. It draws power from two 15STs-45A Ag/Zn (silver/zinc) batteries connected in parallel with the generator and is designed unfailingly to start engines in Siberian winter.

Underwing pylon with K-13A air-to-air missile. (Yefim Gordon)

Two transformers, PO-1500VT-2I and PO-750A, provide single-phase 115V power at 400Hz, and two more, PT-500Ts and PT-125Ts, provide three-phase supplies at 36V, 400Hz. These serve all avionics and instrumentation, lighting (the main landing lights hinge down from underside of wing), armament controls, and windscreen de-icing.

Pneumatic

Two systems, General and Emergency, both charged by an engine-driven air compressor to pressures varying with service, reduce valves giving outputs at 1.02 or 1.56 MPa. The General system serves the wheel brakes, canopy seal, canopy actuation ram, canopy anti-ice/demist, VKK-6 pilot anti-g suit, gun cocking, and braking parachute operation. The Emergency system serves the landing gear extension and wheel brakes. Air bottles are capable of being recharged in the air or from ground supply.

Oxygen

Oxygen comes via an independent KKO-5 gaseous system, fed from six bottles in the wing root to serve the pilot flight suit and the GSh-6 hermetically sealed helmet.

It is operated manually or automatically at high altitude and in case of emergency.

Fire protection

Fire protection is divided into the IS-2MS warning system. It is triggered by sensing rings in the engine bay. It has thermocouples on each side at the front of the bay near the cooling inlets. It also has extinguisher bottles (in the bottom of the engine bay on the right beside ventral fin) and a distribution system. The fire protection system is usable on the ground or in flight.

Equipment

Basic avionics include R-802V (RSIU-5V) VHF communications radio; ARK-10 auto radio compass under nose with GIK goniometer blisters each side of fin; MRP-56P marker beacon receiver; RV-UM or RV-3 low-range radio altimeter (indicating from 0 to 600 m), with dipole antenna under right wing

tip, and in MiG-21F-13 under both tips; SOD-57M air traffic control decimetric transponder; SRO-2 Khrom IFF, with triple rod antennas under nose and above fin; Sirena-D radar warning receiver, with antenna looking back from top of fin; ASP-5ND gun-sight fed with target range measured by SRD-5 simple radar in nose cone; AKS-5 combat camera in upper strut carrying inlet center-body; PVD air data boom with yaw vanes hinged under nose; a small stand-by pressure and total temperature sensor above right side of nose; and ARU-3V artificial-feel system with its own ram inlet on left side of dorsal fin.

Armament

Internal armament is two NR-30 cannons, each firing 30 mm projectiles (average mass 410 g, nearly 1 lb) at a cyclic rate of 900 rounds per minute with a muzzle velocity of 780 m (2,559 ft) per second. Guns were each fed by a short 30-round belt in the magazine between the engine air duct and outer skin above wing. The spent links were collected and empty cases ejected through a slot beside the tank pylon. Under each wing two threaded bosses enabled various interface pylons to be attached to carry: DZ-57 latches for bombs from FAB-50 (kg) to FAB-500 size; same carriers for UB-16-57U launchers for 16 spin-stabilized air-to-air rockets of type S-5M, ARS-57M, or 16 air-to-ground rockets of type S-5K, KARS-57; same carriers for single ARS-240 or S-24 air-to-ground rockets of 240 mm caliber; two PLAB napalm tanks; or (from 1960) APU-13 launch rails for K-13 or improved K-13A (R-3S) infra-red homing missiles, with effective range of from 1 to 7 km (0.62 to 4.35 miles).

MiG-21F air intake. Note two nose cone positions. (Yefim Gordon archive)

GETTING 5 IT RIGHT

The first batch of series aircraft was delivered from Gorkiy in autumn 1959. This initial production version was the simplest, lightest, and cheapest to buy. It was also the nicest to fly, the most agile, and because it had the lowest drag it went the furthest on each unit mass of fuel. Unfortunately, the first version was the least effective in operation, and it later became complicated, heavier, and more expensive. This process continued for more than 30 years. The engine design bureau, led in 1955–'73 by S. K. Tumanskiy, and today called *Soyuz* (Alliance), strove to provide more power without significantly changing the size of engine. This chapter covers the first major production version and a number of early experimental prototypes. In 1959 work was authorized on a trainer version for the MiG-21, judged to be a challenging aircraft for an inexperienced pilot. The first Ye-6U trainer prototype was flown on 17 October 1960.

After Gorkiy had built 30 aircraft in 1959, followed by 69 in the first half of 1960, there was a brief interruption, after which production began again with minor differences. The new aircraft was called the MiG-21F-13 (OKB designation Type 74). The chief modification was removal of the left gun and addition of underwing APU-13 launchers for the K-13 missile. Both had been tested on earlier aircraft. Ye-6T/1 "31" had the left gun removed, and all the Ye-6T prototypes had two missiles and one gun. MiG-21F "51" had one gun, and "93" had one gun and two missiles. All these aircraft were used for extensive armament testing, together with standard MiG-21F "01" used for bombing trials.

A second modification in the MiG-21F-13, on the 115th Gorkiy-built aircraft, was to increase internal fuel capacity by fitting both the front and rear pairs of integral wing tanks and equipping the centerline pylon to carry either the 490-liter (107 gallon) or a larger 800-liter (175 gallons) drop tank. The SRD-5 gun-sight ranging radar was replaced by the SRD-5M *Kvant* (Quantum). For reconnaissance missions an AFA-39 camera could be installed aft of the nosewheel.

Large numbers of MiG-21F and F-13 fighters were assigned to test and evaluation programs. On 9 July 1961 an impressive Aviation Day airshow was held at Moscow Tushi-no, and numerous MiG-21F/F-13s and related aircraft took part, including a vic formation carrying K-13 missiles, although no operational unit existed. The first unit, equipped solely with late-production MiG-21F-13s, was the 28th Regiment based at Odessa. The new fighter's excellent handling was now well known, nobody was particularly bothered by its limited capability, its practical endurance restricted to about 1-1/2 hours, and a lack of search radar. It was enough for its pilots to feel confident in climbing higher and flying faster with greater agility than any known enemies.

Output of the MiG-21F-13 at Gorkiy numbered 132 aircraft in 1960, 272 in 1961, and 202 in the first part of 1962, when it was terminated and replaced by the substantially different MiG-21PF. Another modification introduced in 1960 (to aircraft No. 74210814) was to extend the leading edge of the fin forwards, with a sharp "vee" profile. Yaw (directional) stability had never been a serious problem, except that any sudden turn could result in severe engine malfunction, a violent compressor stall, and even reversal of airflow in the inlet duct. Little

Externally almost indistinguishable from the Ye-6/3, this MiG-21F came from the pre-series batch built at Gorkiy in 1958. It is seen at Zhukovskii, without callsign number. (RSK MiG)

Close up of Red 31, *the Ye-6T/1 at Zhukovskii. (Yefim Gordon archive)*

Taxying past Tupolev Tu-4 Bulls (Boeing B-29 Superfortress copies) at Zhukovskii, the callsign Red 31 *can just be discerned on the Ye-6T/1. (Yefim Gordon archive)*

could be done about this problem in the vertical plane, encountered when "pulling g," but the larger fin significantly reduced excursions in yaw. Later versions were to have still larger fins, and 20 years later the Kiev VVS Institute was to test a completely redesigned inlet.

The second factory, Znamya Truda, began delivering export aircraft in the summer of 1960. These were initially to Egypt, Cuba, India, China, Finland, Poland, East Germany (DDR), Czechoslovakia, Hungary, Iraq, and Indonesia. Czechoslovakia

The Ye-6T/1 (or "Ye-66A") modified for the world air speed record with additional fuel tankage in the spine and rocket engine. (Yefim Gordon archive)

Red 31, *the Ye-6T/1 masquerading as the "Ye-66A" with a more powerful turbojet and an added Dushkin rocket engine, en route to the world height record.*

worked closely with the MiG design bureau, and easily tooled up the Aero Vodochody National Corporation to produce the locally designated S-106. The first few Czech-built

aircraft were almost identical to the standard MiG-21F-13, but the transparent fairing behind the canopy was replaced with a metal panel in the later-built aircraft. The transparency had not significantly improved rearward vision, and it was soon deleted from all subsequent Soviet versions.

In early 1961 a license for the MiG-21F-13 and its RD-11F-300 engine was sold to The People's Republic of China. Two pattern aircraft and some component knocked down (CKD) kits were delivered prior to the cultural split between the two countries. Chinese development of the resulting J-7 and subsequent versions is covered later. This was completely independent of the Soviet Union.

To the MiG-21 program overall, the most important modification in the Ye-66A – the rebuilt Ye-6T/1, *Red 31* – was an added fuel tank of 170 liters (37.4 gallons) in the top of the fuselage a short distance behind the cockpit, between frame Nos. 14 and 17. The canopy was slightly modified by being raised at the rear. This considerably changed the aircraft's appearance. Tunnel testing of models showed little increase in drag, and this initial

Two of the first series MiG-21F fighters were used for NII-VVS bombing trials. Callsign "01" with FAB-100 bombs and aircraft "02" with FAB-500s. Square paving shows "01" was photographed at Zhukovskii; NII paving is in hexagonal slabs. (Yefim Gordon archive)

Two views of one of the first MiG-21F fighters, converted to F-13 standard with left gun removed, on test with K-13 missiles at LII Zhukovskii. (RSK MiG)

increase in volume ahead of the wing improved area ruling. This was a feature of the next production version, the MiG-21PF.

Brute thrust was required to break records. The engine was changed to the RD-11F2-300, which, like the extra tank, was to be a feature of the next series version. Maximum airflow was increased to 65 kg (143 lbs) per second, giving maximum dry and afterburning ratings of 3,950 and 6,120 kg (8,710 and 13,490 lbs), respectively. Underneath an external booster rocket, similar in principle to those used on several mixed-power experimental MiG aircraft of the SM family, was attached. Called a U-21, the demountable package comprised a Dushkin S-3-20M5A rocket engine, with its nozzle inclined 8° downwards, together with its tanks for red fuming nitric acid and HTP propellants.

The pointed-nose rocket pack was mounted on a shallow pylon almost extending along its full

Outboard of the anti-flutter weights the Ye-6T/3 foreplanes were painted, it is believed black/yellow. Just inboard of the wing fences are SOD antennae. (RSK MiG)

The Ye-6T/3, the third series aircraft, was modified to test foreplanes. Note the tracked-vehicle marks in the snow. (RSK MiG)

The foreplanes hardly show in this view of the Ye-6T/3, but the new flush fin-cap radio antenna does, with the GIK-1 sensor just below it. (RSK MiG)

Missile-armed Ye-6T/3 showing its canards. (RSK MiG)

View of the Ye-6T/3 from above. (RSK MiG)

length. It was attached to structurally reinforced frame Nos. 16 and 28. The central ventral fin was replaced by shorter twin canted fins, deeper (410 mm/16 in) than the original, with a combined area of 2.65 m² (28.5 ft²). The fin leading-edge was sharpened still further, increasing area to 4.44 m² (47.7 ft²). On 28 April 1961 Mosolov took *Red 31* in a zoom climb to its dynamic ceiling at 34,714 m (113,891 ft) to set a new record for absolute altitude. As had been done with previous Soviet records, in the submission to the FAI the location was given as "Podmoskovnoye" (this should have been spelled Podmoskovnyi). Western reports translated this as "Podmoskovnoye aerodrome," not realizing that the word merely meant "in the Moscow district." The actual airfield was LII-MAP Zhukovskiy. Twelve years later it was beaten by another OKB pilot, A. V. Fedotov, flying a MiG Ye-155 prototype, reported to the FAI as the Ye-266.

While the Ye-6T/2 was fitted with new wings, the Ye-6T/3 was the first of several MiG experimental aircraft to have canards. MiG OKB and TsAGI had long believed that agility might improve by reducing longitudinal stability. This could be done by moving the center of gravity to the rear, or by adding a destabilizing canard on the front. Following preliminary model testing in high-speed tunnels, the Ye-6T/3 was given small canard surfaces of delta shape with leading-edge angle 45° and cropped tips, and with long

The Ye-6V/2 had a large parabrake under the rudder and a sprung tailwheel, which is seen here extended, as is the rear airbrake. (RSK MiG)

The Ye-6V/2 is seen here with takeoff rockets, centerline tank, and K-13 missiles, but the airbrake and tailwheel are retracted. (RSK MiG)

Close-up of Ye-6V/2 with tank, missiles, and SU-1500 takeoff rockets. (RSK MiG)

forward-pointing mass balance and anti-flutter masses at mid-span. This was the first supersonic canard-equipped aircraft in the USSR. Results were disappointing, but a similar scheme was flown later on the Ye-8. After its test program, the Ye-6T/3 was used as a testbed for guided missile launch systems.

In the late 1950s many air forces became aware that air bases were vulnerable. Both NATO and the Soviet Union studied jet-lift V/STOL (vertical or short takeoff and landing) as a means of dispersing assets. From late 1960, special attention was paid to enabling the MiG-21 to operate from short unprepared strips. This research led to the jet-lift 23-31 (MiG-21PD). The VVS had issued a requirement that all fighters were to be tested on rough unpaved airstrips and snow. This was a severe requirement, and though a little cine film exists, no photographs of these trials have been discovered. Several design bureaux took part, but none succeeded in designing a good retractable ski system.

There were two chief shapes of ski tested. The first tests, between May and July 1960, were made with the Ye-5/2. Prolonged ground testing gave patchy results, directional

stability being poor. Following flight tests led to a switch to a simpler KL (wheel/ski) gear, but this did not enter service. The KL was tested on the Ye-6V/1. This was the first of two Gorkiy-built Type 74 (MiG-21F-13) fighters with the increased chord fin, which were specially modified for STOL testing. They received the designation Ye-6V. By far the most extensive modification was to fit SPS blown flaps, but

The Ye-6V/2 with takeoff rocket booster installation under the rear fuselage, port, and starboard. (RSK MiG)

Ye-6V/2 receives some attention. The fairing for the parabrake under the fin/rudder is apparent. (RSK MiG)

Rear view of the Ye-6V/2. The sprung tailwheel can be seen extended from the rear fuselage strake. (RSK MiG)

Rocket-assisted takeoff by the Ye-6V/2 at the 1961 Tushino show. (Yefim Gordon archive)

Three missile-armed MiG-21F-13s, numbers "04," "28," and "40," took part in the Tushino Aviation Day on 9 July 1961. Until this show, Western analysts believed the MiG-21 to be the swept-wing Faceplate. (Yefim Gordon archive)

An early production MiG-21F-13, with APU-13 missile launchers and a single NR-30 gun on the right side. (Yefim Gordon archive)

for the initial trials this system was inoperative. To reduce takeoff distance, the fuselage was modified to take two *uskoritel* (accelerator) rockets. These were of a standard production type, the SU-1500, with a solid filling and a nozzle canted downwards and outwards, giving an average thrust of 3.5 tons for 10 seconds. Results were impressive, and on Aviation Day, 9 July 1961, Fedotov was airborne in the Ye-6V/2 in an estimated 200 m (656 ft). A photograph taken near the start of the run on this occasion shows the tailplanes at their maximum negative angle, raising the nose as quickly as possible. A number of MiG-21F-13 fighters tested this technique in VVS service.

Reducing the landing run required more thought. The three wheel brakes were already close to their effective limit. Apart from blown flaps, effort was directed towards a high angle-of-attack

approach and to increasing the drag of the parabrake. Both of the Ye-6V aircraft were fitted with two parabrake chutes. Was housed in the normal position and the other placed in an entirely new location immediately below the rudder. It was not intended to stream both chutes together, but to compare the results obtained with each. It was found that the higher position enabled the chute to be streamed before touchdown and a shorter run. Subsequently the higher location became standard. The Ye-6V/1 was later used to test different canopy designs.

The high-AoA testing put the burden on the pilot. In service, the VVS recommended making the landing approach at an AoA of 10° to 11°, but in Ye-6V testing the angle was set at 16° to 18°. On some landings the flaps were locked fully down. To protect the ventral fin it was fitted with a

retractable spring-loaded solid-tired tailwheel. These landings did not take place until July through August 1963, by which time several further MiG-21 versions had entered production. The pilots found the technique difficult and potentially dangerous. The VVS concluded that this was an unacceptable technique, and normal approach using blown flaps was preferred.

Air-to-air picture of a MiG-21F-13. The black smoke is coming from a small container under the right wing. This may be a smoke-generator, but it looks like an ARS-57 rocket launcher. (Yefim Gordon archive)

FIT FOR A MISSION

Though the MiG-21F-13 fully met the original 1953 demand for an agile day air-combat fighter with superior flight performance, it had no radar, except for the simple SRD-5M element of the gun-sight. This was intended only for the measuring range to close targets, to assist accurate gun aiming and ranging for K-13 missiles in good weather. The IA-PVO had to defend the world's largest country, with a frontier 15,850 km (9,850 miles) long. An interceptor version of the MiG-21 was essential. The obvious answer was to try to fit the MiG-21 with effective search radar. In the mid-1950s several radar KBs

At Zhukovskii near sunset, Red 71, the Ye-7/1, was the first of the interceptors. Unusually its fin cap antenna was of black glass fiber. Note the K-13 missiles, PVD boom hinged under the nose, and small wingtip pods. (RSK MiG)

View from above of the Ye-7/1 interceptor prototype, Red 71. *(RSK MiG)*

Red 72, *the second interceptor prototype, Ye-7/2. (Yefim Gordon archive)*

had installations suitable for small jet fighters, the most important being the *Sapfir* (Sapphire) family.

In late 1957, the MiG OKB began full-scale development of the Ye-7, a MiG-21 fitted with Sapfir radar, though paper studies had run into severe forward center-of-gravity (cg) problems. However, a solution became possible by removing the gun. In 1958–'59 the MiG OKB's factory No. 155 built three Ye-7 prototypes based on the Ye-6T, but with airframes re-stressed to the higher load factor of 7.8, a completely new nose, and enlarged main landing wheels. They required significant large blisters above the wing and in the wheel bay door. The right-hand gun and the two fairings were removed. Their absence simplified the design of the forward airbrakes, which were each enlarged to 0.422 m² (4.54 ft²). Frame Nos. 25 and 28 were modified for the attachment of two SU-1500 assisted takeoff rockets, as tested on the two Ye-6V prototypes. The first concession was made to electronic complexity by adding (not at first fitted to Ye-7/1) the KAP-1 autopilot, a single-axis system with authority in roll only.

A basic objective with the Ye-7 prototypes was to produce a fighter capable of some autonomous operation – able to engage at night or in adverse weather. This required more than just short-range radar, and a *kompleks* (an integrated electronic system) was assembled for the future MiG-21 interceptor, to be designated MiG-21P (from *Perekhvatchik*, interceptor). Limited endurance problems could not be overcome in so small an aircraft, though over the years more fuel was added. The size limitation meant the MiG-21P was still going to need ground guidance to a point within 10 km (6 miles), preferably astern, of its target. Finally, the MiG-21P could not land in blind conditions.

Despite these limitations, the fitting of the new *kompleks* would obviously multiply the effectiveness of

The second interceptor, Red 72, *had a colored nose cone, painted inlet lip, silver fin cap antenna, and smaller red star on the fin. (Yefim Gordon archive)*

what by 1960 was locally accepted as probably the best close air combat fighter in the world. Adding radar and AAMs seemed essential to build up an export business. The MiG-21P promised to be what several key foreign customers – especially India – had been asking for, except the lack of a gun.

The key element in the MiG-21P was the radar. The production version for the MiG-21 was to be designated RP-21. Features included a single parabolic antenna of about 550 mm (22 in) diameter, mechanically scanned in a raster (or zig-zag) form through ±30° in azimuth (30° left to 30° right) while searching through a vertical angular distance which could be as great as ±60°, but normally extended from 15° above the aircraft's longitudinal axis to 15° below.

Accommodating the radar meant a very large increase in the size of the inlet center-body. As there was no change in the engine, the maximum airflow remained 65 kg (143 lbs) per second. To pass this around, the larger center-body required an increase in the diameter of the inlet from 690 to 870 mm (34-1/4 in). It also demanded an increase in fuselage length, the distance from the inlet lip to the tail nozzle rising from 12,177 mm to 12,290 mm (40 ft 3-7/8 in).

Head-on view of Ye-7/2 with what looks like Ostapenko in the cockpit. The inlet diameter of 870 mm (2 ft 10-1/4 in) was almost the same as that of the fuselage. (Yefim Gordon archive)

A MiG-21PF, Red 02, showing the new under-nose location of the lower-hemisphere SRO-2 antenna. (RSK MiG)

Production series Ye-7, the first of the MiG-21PFs, at LII-VVS, Zhukovskii. (RSK MiG)

An unidentified Ye-7SPS with PVD boom above the nose and parabrake under the rudder. It is seen here on display (possibly at OKB-155) with a selection of weapons and tanks. (RSK MiG)

The center-body fixed portion was based upon rings of magnesium alloy. These carried the needle roller bearings for the sliding beams that carried the translating cone, now so important that its external profile was made of Oswatitsch type. It was installed with its axis pointing 3° down relative to the longitudinal axis of the fuselage. This was calculated to be the optimum compromise for maximum pressure recovery at all AoA.

As before, the cone was translated hydraulically according to Mach number, but because of its greater size the system was replaced by the more powerful UVD-2M. To cool the radar, a bleed ring surrounded the base of the cone through which

boundary-layer air was sucked by aft-facing ejectors above and below the nose. Normally this airflow cooled the radar, but at Mach numbers over 1.35 it could be shut off by valves, the ram air at such speeds was too hot to be useful. No MiG-21 was expected to hold supersonic speeds for long, due to limited fuel capacity. The Ye-7/1, *Red 71*, was first flown by Ostapenko on 10 August 1958. It had an inert mass to simulate the radar. Most of the other modifications were incorporated, though, like the Ye-7/2, the vertical tail was the original small chord type. The tests, mainly concerned with proving the new inlet, went on successfully until 28 November 1959. A supersonic stall caused the

E-7/1 to spin and toss violently, with alternating g-forces. The aircraft entered an inverted spin, and test pilot Kravtsov bailed out. The E-7/1 disintegrated completely on impact caused by a loss of lateral stability.

Ye-7/2 was completed in 1958 but did not fly until 18 January 1960. Ostapenko and Igor M. Kravtsov completed constructor's flight-testing on 8 May 1960. They considered the new version a satisfactory aircraft, but there were indications of poor radar reliability. All versions of TsD-30 were traditional radars filled with thermionic valves (vacuum tubes).

The Ye-7/3 was fitted with the RD-11F2-300 engine and introduced a modified tail, later to become standard, in which the parts of the final ring were stiffened by extra strips of high-nickel alloy. It also had the broader fin, which by 1961 was the production standard, and the parabrake chute above the jet pipe. All three aircraft had modified fin tips for experiments with radio antennae flush with the structure.

Production of the MiG-21P began at Gorkiy in June 1960, only a month after the completion of OKB testing with the first two Ye-7 prototypes. The radar served little purpose air-to-ground, but the pilot had an optical collimator designated PKI-1 that, in such missions, could be used as a simple optical sight. Only a very limited number were built. Indeed the designation MiG-21P was general-

A series MiG-21PF, with the intermediate fin and original under-fuselage parabrake box and engine nozzle. Note the aft-facing bleed exit above the nose. (RSK MiG)

A MiG-21PFS fairly leaps off the runway by way of of its two SU-1500 rockets. It has the modified engine nozzle and high parabrake tube. (Yefim Gordon archive)

Late in life, even this early MiG-21PF was camouflaged. Photographed around 1980 with a VVS training unit. (Yefim Gordon archive)

ly taken in the OKB to refer to the Ye-7 prototypes. Thus, the next series production aircraft was the MiG-21PF.

Short range and endurance remained unaddressed, fuel capacity being 2,380 liters (523.5 gallons). By 1961 the successful testing of the Ye-66A showed the feasibility of an extra tank in the top of the fuselage. The OKB developed this further, finding a way to add two tanks totaling 370 liters (81.3 gallons), and these were incorporated in the Ye-7/4, flown in August 1962. Total internal capacity thus became 2,750 liters (605 gallons). This required the re-profiled canopy, large metal rear fairing and repositioned VHF mast. The Ye-7/4 was also the first to have the new PVD-5 boom, mounted as a non-pivoted fixture at the top of the nose inlet, where pilots found it a useful indicator of AoA and drift. It was also the first MiG-21 to be fitted with *Khrom-Nikel* (chrome-nickel) SRO-2M IFF, the downward-hemisphere antenna being moved forward.

Red 04 *was one of the small batch of MiG-21PFS. It has the extension strips at top and bottom of the nozzle. (Yefim Gordon archive)*

Further Ye-7 development aircraft followed, all powered by the RD-11F2-300 engine, and all with the broad fin. There were many other detail changes, particularly associated with SPS (*Sduva Pogranichnovo Sloya* – boundary layer blower system or blown flaps), though few were visible externally.

Ye-7/4 was later fitted with the broad fin, and undertook the first tests with the AoA indicator mounted on the left side. This took the form of a simple weathercock vane on a horizontal shaft driving an electric potentiometer position sensor, mounted outboard to place it beyond the boundary layer. Many

A cutaway Tumanskii R-11F2S-300, surrounded by instructional displays. The large disc amidships on a perforated ring is one of the bleed connections. (Yefim Gordon archive)

An official side view of a Type 77, prototype of the broad-fin MiG-21PFM. It has long-nose R-3R missiles and the PVD boom above the nose, but the original parabrake installation. (RSK MiG)

Red 22, a series MiG-21PFM, Type 77, with broad fin and parabrake under the rudder. It re-introduced the black fin cap antenna. (RSK MiG)

pilots had urgently asked for such a sensor that linked to a cockpit instrument that could be seen easily during a landing approach, but it was not to reach production until the MiG-21R of 1965. The Ye-7/8 tested the reconnaissance pods fitted to the MiG-21R, and also wing pylons plumbed for 490-liter external tanks.

The more powerful RD-11F2-300 engine and RP-21 radar changed the service designation to MiG-21PF, *Izdeliye* 76. At the beginning of 1962, while Ye-7 testing at LII-VVS Zhukovskiy was still incomplete, orders were placed for series production at Gorkiy, and a considerable number – far greater than for the MiG-21F and F-13 – were built by

1964 for both Frontal Aviation and also for some regiments in the IA-PVO. PVO aircraft were located at bases nearest to likely threats, where their short range was less significant.

A further substantial number were delivered from the Znamya Truda factory in 1964–'68. These export batches began with Poland and East Germany, continuing with

Takeoff by a MiG-21PFM Type 94, with KM-1 seat and side-hinged canopy with fixed windscreen. (Yefim Gordon archive)

India, Yugoslavia, Egypt, Ethiopia, and Sudan, followed by North Vietnam, North Korea, North Yemen, and Cuba. Most of these aircraft had minor changes in avionics, usually to omit certain items or replace them by older patterns that had been downgraded in security classification. The Vietnamese batch received the designation MiG-21PF-V, having the structure and equipment protected against high temperature and humidity.

After it had finished its test programs, one Ye-7, reported to the FAI as the Ye-76, was used in 1966–'67 to set a number of women's records. These comprised: 16 September 1966 Marina Solovyeva set a 500-km closed-circuit record at 2,062 km/h (1,281 mph); 11 October 1966 Yevginia Martova flew a 2,000-km circuit at 900.26 km/h (559.4 mph); 18 February 1967 Martova flew a 100 km circuit at 2,128.7 km/h (1,322.75 mph); and on 28 March 1967 Lydia Zaitseva flew a 1,000-km circuit at 1,298.16 km/h (806.7 mph). In each case the engine was given as the Type 37F, rated at 5,950 kg (13,117 lbs), 50 kg less than the figure reported in 1961 for the Type 37F fitted to the Ye-66A. The 500-km circuit, taking a full 15 minutes, was clearly flown with maximum afterburner.

As early as 1957 both the MiG OKB and TsAGI were studying ways of increasing low-speed lift without increasing wing size, and flap blowing was regarded as the likely solution. Pioneered in the USA, hot high-pressure air is bled from the engine and discharged as a very thin sheet from narrow slits just above and ahead of the flap. This results in a considerable increase in lift. Not only does it assist lift, but, by forcing the airflow to stay "attached" to the flap, instead of stalling and breaking away in turbulent eddies, the maximum flap angle can be considerably increased. Bleeding a large airflow from a jet engine means that that much less air is available to enter the combustion chamber and turbine. If the flow of fuel is unaltered then the gas temperature at the turbine will go "off

the clock" and the turbine blades will fail. Therefore, the fuel flow has to be reduced in proportion.

By sheer chance, the MiG-21 proved to be almost ideal for flap blowing. The bleed connections of the installed engine were within a few inches of the inboard end of the rear wing spar ahead of the flap. The blowing slit was made of heat-resistant steel and attached to the rear auxiliary spar between rib Nos.1 and 6. Standard gap between the blowing slit and the extended flap is 2.2 ± 0.2 mm. The flaps themselves were slightly smaller, having a projected area of 0.92 m² (9.9 ft²) instead of 0.935 m², and instead of running out on tracks they were simply hinged. Each flap was actuator driven with chambers in both full-pressure hydraulic systems, which pulled the surface down by a bracket near the leading edge at mid-span. Normal angles are 25° for takeoff and 45° for landing. The flaps could be used in combat, balancing their deflection angle against air load at speeds above 400 km/h (248 mph) until at 700 km/h (435 mph) deflection is zero.

The MiG-21 SPS system worked well and hardly changed during three years of exhaustive testing on the Ye-7SPS. A reason for the long delay in production was the violent reaction on selecting SPS operative.

From 1960 pilots of the IA-PVO, unlike those of Frontal Aviation, wore partial-pressure suits and sealed helmets. (Russian Aviation Research Trust)

The first HAL-built Type 77 MiG-21FL in 1966. (Russian Aviation Research Trust)

Lowering the flaps to the landing position had always caused a nose-down trim change, but selecting full SPS flap – holding the stick loosely neutral – resulted in the aircraft ballooning through some 200 m (656 ft), while at the same time rotating nose-down. The breathtaking gain in height was immediately followed by an equally rapid loss of height. The difficulty of arresting the sink with full-blown flap eventually resulted in VVS standard procedure being to land with only 25° (takeoff) flap, which, to a large extent, negated the object of the exercise.

SPS entered Gorkiy production in 1964, the resulting aircraft being designated MiG-21PFS. By this time, flap blowing had been tested on several Ye-7s and a MiG-21U, and it was featured on all subsequent production MiG-21 versions. Nevertheless, for a long time the SPS system in VVS-line-service MiG-21s was locked inoperative. By the time SPS was incorporated, several further modifications were about to be introduced, and only a few PFS aircraft were built, all going to one regiment. Thus, about a month later in 1964, Gorkiy switched to making the MiG-21PFM, initially *Izdeliye* 77. The pronounced broader vertical tail increased the total area of fin and rudder to a remarkable 5.32 m^2 (57.27 ft^2). Apart from minor variations caused by changes in the spine, this was to be the fin size for all subsequent production versions, and it significantly cut down the number of violent in-flight engine stalls and flameouts caused by transient excursions in yaw.

To expand the possible range of weapon fits, the radar was replaced by the RP-21M. This had a guidance function for compatible radar command-guided missiles, notably the RS-2US (K-51) AAM, which was rapidly approaching obsolescence and the Kh-23 (*Kompleks* 66) for precision attack of surface targets. This dramatically improved the aircraft's versatility, but many pilots preferred a gun. An excellent new gun was packaged together with its cooling, control system, and a 200-round magazine into a removable pack with the designation GP-9. The self-powered and electrically fired GSh-23 was able to fire 23-mm ammunition with high velocity from twin barrels at the cyclic rate of 3,600 rounds/min. This could be scabbed on the underside of the mid-fuselage. An improved sight was fitted, the ASP-PF-21, also called simply PKI. The Samotsvet infrared sight served for night target detection and use of all weapons in good weather, irrespective of the flight altitude. Other modifications included the introduction of *Khrom-Nikel* SRO-2M IFF and Sirena-3M radar warning, mounted on each side of the fin. For short takeoffs it was possible to attach an SPRD-99 rocket on each side of the fuselage, secured to the anchorages previously used for the more powerful SU-1500. The thrust of each rocket was 2.5 tons (5,511 lbs) for up to 17 seconds. These rockets were used in VVS service.

A simplified version of the MiG-21PFM was prepared for

license-construction at Hindustan Aeronautics Ltd (HAL), in India. Whereas the Indian Air Force had used the MiG-21F-13, all these had been imported from the Soviet Union. Organizing production of the fighter in India, under an agreement signed in 1962, was a colossal task involving a new group of factories at *Koraput* (engines), *Hyderabad* (avionics and instruments), and *Nasik* (airframe, final assembly and flight test). The initial version (designated MiG-21FL, Type 77) featured the RD-11F-300 engine, simpler R-2L radar, and greater fuel capacity of 2,900 liters (637.9 gallons). Initial aircraft, followed by CKD kits for Indian assembly, were produced in Moscow in 1965–'68 for production in 1966–'73.

Production of the MiG-21PFM for the VVS began at Gorkiy in late 1964. At the 15th aircraft a new design of seat became available. This outstanding seat, the KM-1, still could not be used at below 130 km/h (81 mph), but it could be fired at up to 1,200 km/h (745 mph) indicated airspeed, and at any height. It proved to be very reliable, and the canopy was redesigned with a strong fixed windscreen and a separate main canopy hinged to open sideways to the right.

The MiG-21PFM was to have been the new standard aircraft, but only a year later it was replaced on the production line by still newer versions. The Znamya Truda factory produced export versions between 1966–'68.

A NEW GENERATION

By 1960, before any MiG-21s were in operational service, the MiG OKB could see a series of possible improvements and modifications. Aerodynamics and flight control were judged outstanding, and as early as 1957 the problems posed by fitting search radar were essentially solved.

Almost all the other pressures for change were concerned with engine thrust, weapons, and, especially, internal fuel capacity. However, the third-generation family started with a totally different role.

In the late 1950s Frontal Aviation had plenty of tactical reconnaissance aircraft, mainly the large

Ilyushin Il-28R Beagle and Yakovlev Yak-27R Mangrove. In addition there were a handful of MiG-19R single-seaters with shorter range, but unable to operate at night or in bad weather. What was wanted was a survivable platform that combined supersonic speed with night and all-weather capability. From

The first reconnaissance MiG-21 was Ye-7/8, the eighth Ye-7 prototype. It combined the old MiG-21PFS airframe with the new parabrake installation, a unique round-topped fin cap antenna, and five pylons shown here loaded with a Type-R pod, two tanks, and two R-3S missiles. (RSK MiG)

Ye-7/8 head-on, showing the PVD boom moved to the right side; the wing tip electronic warfare antenna containers can also be seen clearly. Inboard pylons are fitted but empty. (RSK MiG)

A series MiG-21R, Type 94R, with KM-1 seat and new canopy, spine, fin, and cap antenna, wing tip receiver antenna pods, and AoA sensor on the left side of the nose. It is carrying a Type-D pod, and (as was common) has the inboard pylons removed. (RSK MiG)

MiG-21R Red 22, seen from below carrying two tanks and a D-type pod. The wing-tip antenna pods stand out clearly. (Yefim Gordon archive)

1955 the OKB of P. V. Tsybin had been developing the RSR, a reconnaissance aircraft able to fly at great heights at nearly Mach 3 (a predecessor of the Lockheed SR-71 Blackbird). This was more strategic in nature, and likely to be very costly, and in 1959–'61 its funds were transferred to strategic missiles just before first flight. Frontal Aviation could never have operated anything as complex as the Tsybin RSR.

Mikoyan was convinced that the need could be met by a new version of the MiG-21, to be designated MiG-21R (*Razvedchik*, reconnaissance). Studies for such an aircraft began in the late 1950s, requiring minimal changes to the airframe. The reconnaissance sensors were to be carried under the centerline in a streamlined container. To replace the centerline drop tank, the wings would be plumbed for four underwing drop tanks. Aerodynamic drag would obviously increase significantly. Speed at very low level would still be about Mach 0.95, while at high altitude it might reach about Mach 1.6. Both figures would be determined by payload limits rather than lack of thrust. Packaging the sensors into a pod would enable various types of pods to be produced for different missions.

The first flight tests were carried out with the Ye-7/8 prototype. Another difference from other early MiG-21PF aircraft was a redesigned fin top made of fiber-reinforced plastics forming a large flush antenna. This curved over at the top to carry a modified streamlined fairing for the other fin top antennas and fuel vent. All four wing-stations were plumbed and tested with four 490-liter (107.8-gallon) tanks. The inboard stations were also wired for AAMs and the pylon could have an APU-13 or APU-13MT interface shoe for, respectively, an R-3R or R-3S self-defense missile. The centerline pylon had a fuel connection, but no weapon capability. It had a multi-pin socket and attachments

Two views of the MiG-21S fighter prototype. The extended spine housed extra fuel, and the aircraft also featured a better radar than earlier versions. (RSK MiG)

for any of four families of sensor pods. The four fixed containers had a pointed nose, irregular shape in side elevation, oval cross section with a flat underside, pylon interface on top, and a shallow dorsal fin at the tail.

The first patterns to be tested, and the most numerous in service, were the D (day), N (night), and R (radio). The D family pods were for daylight optical photography. Each normally accommodated seven cameras, typically six A-39 or AFA-39 and one AShTShAFA-SM for strip coverage that could, if necessary, extend to either horizon. Under the pod's nose was an oblique flat window for a forward-looking camera. The other six cameras were arranged in pairs in three successive heated bays, looking through win-

dows in the flat bottom. In addition most D pods carried SPO-3R passive radar receiver antennas covering 360° in azimuth, as well as radar monitoring and countermeasures, which could include an ASO-2I chaff/flare dispenser. Later D-type pods housed electro-optical (TV) sensors and/or IR linescan. Typical D-series pods weighed 285 kg (628 lbs).

As their "radio" designation prefix suggested, the R-series pods were concerned primarily with electronic surveillance. In all cases a single A-39 camera was carried in the forward oblique position, but the window was further back than in the D-series and set at a shallower angle, giving the pod a smoother outline. Major sensors were sideways-looking airborne radars

(SLARs) of the Lyra family. Comprehensive radio and radar surveillance receivers covering various wavebands were coupled to recorders, usually of the MS-81 type. Either of two types of chaff/flare dispensers were always installed under the aft section.

Two other types of pods were built in series by the time the MiG-21R was in service. The ED type, from *Efer* (ether), was concerned entirely with electronic intelligence (Elint) and communications intelligence (Comint), and housed radio receivers, recorders and countermeasures. The N-series pods were specifically for night photographic sensing, and contained night and IR cameras, again with self-defense countermeasures. All pods were linked to the aircraft's

The MiG-21S, first of the new-generation fighters with RP-22 Sapfir radar and extra spine fuel. The PVD boom is at 12 o'clock. (RSK MiG)

own air data and navigation systems, so that all information brought back could be matched precisely to a location and time.

Following two years of testing, the MiG-21R, with OKB designation Type 94R, was settled in 1964, and substantial orders were placed, far exceeding those for any previous Soviet jet reconnaissance aircraft. Series aircraft were delivered from Gorkiy from 1965–'71. Important further changes were made which qualify the MiG-21R as the first of the new-generation aircraft.

The MiG-21R was fitted with the very broad (5.32 m², 57.2 ft²) fin and with the cruciform braking parachute housed above the jet pipe. The radar remained the RP-21, and the nose was unchanged, except that the AoA indicator was moved. The swollen spine extended all the way to the fin providing additional space for a re-arrangement of radio equipment as well as two 170-liter (37.4-gallon) spine tanks to bring the total internal fuel capacity to 2,800 liters (616 gallons). This increased the range on a typical mission to some 1,600 km (about 1,000 miles) with two external tanks, or 1,130 km on internal fuel only.

Less obvious was the appearance of small streamlined pods carried on short horizontal pylons. They extend beyond the wingtips housing the passive antennas of the SPO-3 system for detecting and locating hostile radars and other emitters. The system provided 360° azimuth coverage with an overlap on each side providing a reconnaissance sensor and a self-protective system. A welcome modification was the installation of a full-authority three-axis AP-155 autopilot. After 1969 most MiG-21R aircraft were retrofitted with the TS-27AMSh rear-view periscope.

The Type 94R found foreign customers, unusually filled from Gorkiy. Egypt purchased a unique version of the MiG-21RF in which three optical cameras, usually of A-39 type, were fitted internally in a compartment under the floor of the cockpit. Typically, one would be forward oblique and the other two inclined left and right to give overlapping images. They were mounted on a hinged pallet so that the magazines could be changed quickly. The pallet projected as a long but shallow blister behind the nose-gear bay. Cameras in the MiG-21RF occupied a battery compartment in the MiG-21R. An external cable fairing ran from this bay to the centerline pylon. It was possible to convert aircraft from R to RF, and vice versa.

The Type 94's success prompted Mikoyan to produce an updated frontal fighter, the Type 95. This was cleared to the previous structural load factor of 8.5. It combined the extended spine, containing two 340-liter (74.8-gallon) tanks, with a better radar, the RP-22 Sapfir. This fitted the same space but had greater power, giving a range against the standard 16 m² (172 ft²) target of 30 km (18.6 miles) and an effective tail-on pursuit range of 15km (9.3 miles). Most of these features were tested in 1964 on prototypes designated Ye-7S (from Sapfir), and a large order was placed for Frontal Aviation with the designation MiG-21S. These aircraft were delivered

An official picture of the MiG-21SM, Type 95M (Type 15), with R-13-300 engine and internal GSh-23L gun. (RSK MiG)

MiG-21SM seen head-on with inlet cone partly extended, two R-3R and two R-3S missiles, centerline tank, and two SPRD-99 takeoff rockets. (RSK MiG)

from Gorkiy in parallel with the MiG-21R in 1965–'68. Following testing with a prototype designated Ye-7N, the centerline pylon was cleared to carry a tactical nuclear bomb.

These changes unquestionably resulted in an improved fighter, but in some respects performance had deteriorated. This was due to the normal loaded weight rising to 8,150 kg (17,967 lbs), a ton heavier than the MiG-21F-13, with no significant increase in engine power. Obviously there was a need for a more powerful engine, and this was met by Tumanskii with the R-13-300. In parallel, Mikoyan OKB developed an export version of the MiG-21S designated MiG-21M, with *Izdeliye* number of 96. Though this retained the RD-11F2S-300 engine, it introduced several new features, including the radar, gun, sight, and for exports, the offset PVD. The radar was the RP-21MA, coupled to the improved ASP-PFD sight. The greatest advance was the installation of the gun; instead of a GSh-23 installed in a bulky GP-9 external pack, the GSh-23L was mounted on a platform flush with the underside.

This platform could be lowered for reloading or maintenance, but caused very little drag. The magazine lay between frame Nos. 13 and 14, with a belt of 200 (maximum 220) rounds. A steel blast panel was added to the fuselage skin ahead of the muzzles. In the course of production of both this and the MiG-21SM versions, it was discovered that blasts from the muzzles could blow open the auxiliary engine inlets and

The first MiG-21M from Hindustan Aeronautics. This Indian Air Force example is shown carrying four APU-13 rails. (via Russian Aviation Research Trust)

A camouflaged MiG-21MF of the East German LSK, carrying 10 high-drag FAB-100 bombs. (Yefim Gordon archive)

cause violent compressor stalls at high AoA and low airspeed; therefore, a small deflector plate was added below each of these inlets. These plates also helped to prevent the ingestion of dirt and stones during takeoffs from contaminated runways. This internal installation of the gun meant that other loads could still be carried on the centerline pylon, which was immediately behind the gun.

Production of the MiG-21M for numerous foreign air forces took place at Znamya Truda from 1968 to 1971. In 1971 the Indian government was licensed to build the Type 96. The first aircraft was built at Nasik at the end of January 1973 and delivered on 14 February. For

All these Polish MiG-21MF fighters have a mix of APU-4 rails inboard and APU-13 outboard, for RS-2US and R-3R/R-3S missiles respectively. (WAF)

For the campaign of 21 August 1968 to take Prague, and nip in the bud Czechoslovakia's move towards democracy, Soviet aircraft such as this MiG-21SM wore red "invasion stripes." (Yefim Gordon archive)

DIMENSIONS, EXTERNAL (MiG-21 MF):
Wing span . . . . .7.15 m (23 ft 5 1/2 in)
Length, incl pitot boom . . . . .15.76 m (51 ft 8 1/2 in)
Fuselage length, intake lip to jetpipe nozzle . . . . .12.30 m (40 ft 4 1/4 in)
Height overall . . . . .4.10 m (13 ft 5 1/2 in)
Tailplane span . . . . .3.70 m (12 ft 8 in)
Wheel track . . . . .2.69 m (8 ft 10 in)
Wheelbase . . . . .4.81 m (15 ft 9V2 in)
Wings, gross area . . . . .23.0 m2 (247.0 sq ft)

WEIGHTS AND LOADINGS (MiG-21 MF):
Weight empty . . . . .5,843 kg (12,882 lbs)

Take-off weight:
with four K-13A missiles . . . . .8,200 kg (18,078 lbs)
with two K-13A missiles and two 490 liter tanks . . . . .8,950 kg (19,730 lbs)
with two K-13As and three drop tanks . . . . .9,400 kg (20,725 lbs)
Max T-0 weight . . . . .9,800 kg (21,605 lbs)
Max wing loading . . . . .426.0 kg/m2 (87.5 lbs/sq ft)
Max power loading . . . . .151.4 kg/kN (1.48 lbs/lb st)

Performance:
Max level speed: above 11,000 m (36,000 ft) .M2.05 (1,175 kt; 2,175 km/h; 1,353 mph)
at low altitude . . . . .M1.06 (701 kt; 1,300 km/h; 807 mph)
Landing speed . . . . .146 kt (270 km/h; 168 mph)
Design ceiling . . . . .18,000 m (59,050 ft)
Practical ceiling . . . . .about 15,250 m (50,000 ft)
Take-off run at normal AUW . . . . .800 m (2,625 ft)
Landing run . . . . .550 m (1,805 ft)

Combat radius (hi-lo-hi):
with four 250 kg bombs, internal fuel . . . . .200 n miles (370 km; 230 miles)
with two 250 kg bombs and drop tanks . . . . .400 n miles (740 km; 460 miles)
Range, internal fuel only . . . . .593 n miles (1,100 km; 683 miles)
Ferry range, with three external tanks . . . . .971 n miles (1,800 km; 1,118 miles)

Performance (MiG-21 US, clean):
Max level speed above 12,200 m (40,000 ft) .M2.02 (1,159 kt; 2,150 km/h; 1,335 mph)
at sea level . . . . .M1.06 (701 kt; 1,300 km/h; 807 mph)
Max rate of climb at sea level . . . . .6,400 m (21,000 ft)/min
Rate of climb at 11,000 m (36,000 ft) . . . . .3,050 m (10,000 ft)/min
Time to 1,500 m (4,920 ft) . . . . .20 s

Turn rate at 4,575 m (15,000 ft):
instantaneous (M0.5) . . . . .11.1°/s
instantaneous (M0.9) . . . . .13.4°/s
sustained (M0.9) . . . . .7.5°/s
Take-off run . . . . .700 m (2,297 ft)

Takeoff by a MiG-21M, Type 96, of the Czech CL. It has APU-13 rails inboard and APU-4 outboard. (Yefim Gordon archive)

A shot from a well-known staged sequence, but underlining the increased capability of the maturing MiG-21 line. This MiG-21SM of Frontal Aviation is apparently readying for a night sortie. (Russian Aviation Research Trust)

Czech Republic MiG-21R 2133 on finals. (Chris Lofting)

Frontal Aviation, Mikoyan developed the MiG-21SM, whose *Izdeliye* number of 95M was later changed to the out-of-sequence number of 15. This incorporated every available updated feature including the afterburning R-13-300. The MiG-21SM generally resembled the MiG-21M apart from having the latest avionics, including the RP-22 radar and a number of improved cockpit instruments.

The next logical development was an export MiG-21 based on the more powerful engine. With the *Izdeliye* number of 96F, this version was more generally known by the service designation MiG-21MF. An exception was the very similar version made under license by HAL in India, which was the MiG-21M *Izdeliye* 88. Navaids were integrated into a *kompleks* called PNK Pilot-OI, while automatic flight-control was provided by a *kompleks* designated SBU-23YeSN. The MiG-21MF entered production at Znamya Truda in 1970. Early in production the TS-27AMSh rear-view periscope was added, as it was to many existing aircraft of earlier types. The same was true of the offset air-data boom. Like the MiG-21S, SM, and M, the MiG-21MF was fitted with the PVD-7, with the Pion-N (*Peony*) feeder coupler, sensing dynamic pressure, three static pressures and pairs of angular measures of angle of attack, and yaw. The latter, fed by freely pivoted swept-back vanes, helped reduce engine stalls but were required primarily to assist gun aiming. Cockpit instruments were usually fed not by this boom but by the AoA sensor on the left side of the nose and the small pitot on the right side below the windscreen. Following failure of either source, the remaining one could be used to feed the pilot's instruments.

In September 1971 the MiG-21MF was one of the first versions to be studied in the West when two accompanied Chief Marshal of Aviation P. S. Kutakhov on an official visit to Reims, France.

IMPROVING A THOROUGHBRED

In 1969–'70 the Mikoyan designers redesigned the MiG-21 dorsal spine to accommodate still more fuel. The final three-tank arrangement raised the internal fuel capacity to 3,250 liters (715 gallons). The stability margin caused the rearmost tank to be removed, losing 300 liters (66 gallons). There was a significant increase in both drag and weight. Thus, flight performance (rate of climb in particular) was reduced, and takeoff distance increased to almost a kilometer.

The new version was given the OKB product number Type 50, and designation MiG-21SMT. A small number were produced at Gorkiy in 1971–'72, all of them camouflaged and put into limited VVS-FA service.

Most were modified with a narrower spine, thereafter being designated MiG-21ST. An export version with an earlier communications radio was produced as the Type 96T, or MiG-21MT (T from *Toplivo*, fuel). In 1971 the Znamya Truda plant constructed 15 of this version, but none were exported. Five were handed to the VVS test-pilot school, and one was used by the OKB for research.

Tumanskii, led by Gavrilov, had, by 1969, qualified another uprated engine as a bolt-on replacement for earlier versions. This, the R-25-300, had re-bladed LP and HP compressors to give a higher-pressure ratio with improved efficiency. The first LP stage had only 21 titanium blades of increased chord. This enhanced resistance to foreign object damage (FOD). The maximum sustained power without afterburner was set at 4.1 tons (9,040 lbs), but the new two-stage afterburner gave appreciably higher thrust augmentation. The maximum continuous thrust with full reheat at sea level was fixed at 7.1 tons (15,650 lbs), but at Mach numbers equal to or greater

Two official NII-VVS photos of a MiG-21SMT, Blue 05, with a huge spine joining the canopy to the parabrake container. Features include a PVD-7 boom with two-axis vane sensors, Khrom-Nikel IFF (not SRZO), and UB-16-57U rocket launchers. (Yefim Gordon archive)

Two official photographs of the MiG-21bis. (RSK MiG)

MiG-21bis Blue 22 was photographed officially by the NII-VVS. Note the SRZO IFF blade antennae under the nose and above the fin. (Yefim Gordon archive)

than 1.0 a special combat regime – termed ChR – could be engaged for up to three minutes, increasing afterburning thrust to 95 kN (9.69 tons, 21,355 lbs).

This engine promised improved performance, the ChR thrust being roughly double the maximum in early MiG-21 versions. There were strong grounds for ordering a large number of R-25 engines, because it was less sensitive to the inlet air-

flow, and would reduce the frequency of violent compressor stalls and flameouts. Eventually, the engine was ordered in substantial numbers for both the VVS and a number of export customers, but not for retrofitting.

To take the improved engine, the Mikoyan team produced the Type 75 with service designation MiG-21bis (bis translates to "encore" in French and Latin). It was tested from 1969 on a prototype designated Ye-7bis. Externally, the key distinguishing feature was again the dorsal spine. This was at last optimized for usable fuel, set at 2,880 liters (633.5 gallons), or 2,390 kg. Visually, the spine was clearly larger than that of the MiG-21MF, especially near mid-length, but it was not as swollen as that of the MiG-21SMT and it tapered into the fin ahead of the parabrake tube instead of merging into it. Structurally the airframe was largely redesigned. With 17 years of anomalies, it actually proved possible to reduce the airframe weight. Blown flaps and SPRD-99 attachments were unchanged. The few visible modifications included skinning the underside of the forward fuselage with detachable panels and reinforcing the inner front section of the tailplanes.

An important addition was the RSBN-6S short-range navigation system and coupled instrument landing system, with a horizontal rod antenna projecting forwards under the nose. This enabled flights to be made in really bad weather and conditions of extremely poor visibility for the first time. A small number were also built and designated MiG-21bisN, equipped for tactical nuclear weapons. These were carried on the centerline, and required ancillary equipment in the fuselage. The most common weapons remained the GSh-23L gun and various combinations of R-3R/R-3S and pairs of the very agile R-60 or R-60M close-range AAMs. The MiG-21bis was the first version to

MiG-21bis, Blue 07, parked at Akhtubinsk in June 1995. (Yefim Gordon)

MiG-21bis of the Ukrainian Air Force is equipped to the latest avionics standard, with RSBN rod antennas at nose and tail. The winged symbol within the pale blue roundel (with white outline) is hardly visible. (Alfred Matusevich)

MiG-21bis "MG-122" of Finland's HävLv-31, parked with full right rudder. Camouflage is dark and pale green. (Via Yefim Gordon)

Final assembly of Type 75 MiG-21bis fighters at the Nasik plant of Hindustan Aeronautics. With this aircraft HAL strove to become self-sufficient. (HAL)

use the K-13M (R-3M), which could now be fired under any combat g load and whose firing envelope was double that of the original R-3S. The ASP-5ND sight now provided high precision aiming up to +2.9g.

Production MiG-21bis fighters were built between 1972 and '74, and only at Gorkiy. VVS aircraft were designated Type 75P, while export aircraft were designated Type 75A for Warsaw Pact countries and 75B for the rest of the world. One of the first customers from outside the Warsaw Pact was the Ilmavoimat of Finland, which was one of the earliest customers in 1962. In 1973 its test pilots thoroughly evaluated the MiG-21bis, writing a glowing report. Another very important customer was India, which again purchased a manufacturing license. The IAF received 75 Gorkiy-built aircraft, followed by

220 assembled, and increasingly manufactured, at the HAL Nasik Division in 1979–'87.

Other Asian and African air forces also purchased the MiG-21bis, because of its low price, obvious effectiveness, and type of technology. Most export deliveries took place in 1974. By this time the General Dynamics F-16 Fighting Falcon and the Dassault Mirage 2000 were emerging as new technology fighters. Price put these aircraft out of reach of most air forces. With so many aircraft in service with

so many air forces, updating the later types of MiG-21 now became an important business. Production of the MiG-21bis at Gorkiy totaled 2,030 aircraft, ending in October 1974. At that time Tbilisi's production of the MiG-21UM still had six months to go. The total for all versions was 10,158, as shown in the table below:

MiG-21 production

	Gorkiy	Moscow	Tbilisi	Total
Fighters	5,278	3,203	17	8,498
Trainers	—	—	1,660	1,660
			Total	10,158

To these figures can be added 194 MiG-21F-13 made in Czechoslovakia and approximately 2,400 aircraft built in China, giving an overall total exceeding 12,750.

Prior to the 1960s the standard Soviet jet trainer was the MiG-15UTI Midget, a simple, reliable and low-cost stepping stone to operational types. It was, of course, subsonic. In contrast, there were dual trainer versions of all the Sukhoi aircraft in front-line service. When the decision was made to put the MiG-21 – a Mach 2 delta, into production – Mikoyan asked his team to consider a dual-control trainer version, and various studies ensued. The optimum arrangement, *Izdeliye* 66, was launched in November 1959. The Ye-6U/1 prototype was flown by Pyotr M. Ostapenko on 17 October 1960.

It was almost identical with the series MiG-21F, though it was designed to the reduced load factor of 7.0. The fuselage length from inlet to nozzle remained 12.177mm, and the engine was still the RD-11F-300. The fuselage was redesigned between Frames 6 and 22 to accommodate the pupil in the front cockpit and the instructor in an added rear cockpit, but was not raised significantly to improve forward view. SK seats were standard. In front of the pupil was a fixed windshield with a near oval flat front screen. Above each cockpit was a separate long canopy hinged to the right, locked open by a stay. A flat transparent windbreak between the cockpits carried the pressure seals for both canopy edges, but it was not strong enough to serve as a crash arch.

The inlet to the engine duct was unchanged from that of the MiG-21F, but the PVD boom no longer pivoted and was moved to the central position. For gunnery training the SRD-5 ranging radar and ASP-5ND sight were installed, but the devastating NR-30 cannon was removed,

Three official views of the Ye-6U/1 prototype. (RSK MiG)

The Ye-6U/4 was the fourth Type 66 two-seat MiG-21U. It is seen here in use as an LII platform for photo and TV work, in this case flying as chase aircraft to an Su-9U used for ejection seat trials. (Yefim Gordon archive)

replaced when necessary by a pod on the centerline pylon housing a single A-12.7 heavy machine gun. The twin forward airbrakes on the centerline were replaced by a single large one, enhancing deceleration. The main wheels were the larger 700mm type introduced on the Ye-7/MiG-21P, requiring large blisters in the fuselage and doors. The autopilot was the KAP-2, with authority in roll only. The parabrake was in the underside of the fuselage.

Internal fuel capacity actually increased. A large metal fuel tank was inserted between Frame Nos. 14 through 22, extending upwards to occupy the capacious but sharply tapered fairing behind the instructor's canopy, augmenting the five flexible cells between Frame Nos. 14 through 28. Thus, internal fuel rose to 2,350 liters (517 gallons), or 1,950 kg, and further in production aircraft.

The Ye-6U/1, *Red 61*, was soon joined by Ye-6U/2. A telemetry antenna was added under the forward fuselage. Development posed few problems and OKB testing lasted little over nine months. A large order was placed for the series aircraft, designated MiG-21U, Type 66. (*Uchyebnii* – trainer; ASCC reporting

The VVS had little chance to use the MiG-21 in anger – thankfully. This posed photograph shows pilots walking across the vast apron to their machines. A MiG-15UTI can be seen in the background. (Yefim Gordon archive)

A contrived photograph, but it nevertheless shows the two-seat cockpit and side-hinged canopy of MiG-21US Blue 66. (Yefim Gordon archive)

A big fin MiG-21US in service at a VVS pilot school. It has three empty pylons, and one of the blown-flap actuator fairings has caught the sunlight. (Yefim Gordon archive)

This MiG-21US, Type 68, has extra equipment (such as the AoA sensor and instructor periscope) making it look like a MiG-21UM. It has no UHF blade antenna. (Yefim Gordon archive)

name Mongol.) Fresh production capacity had to be found, and the choice fell on Factory No. 31 at Tbilisi, capital of Georgia. Series manufacture began here in 1962, terminating with No. 180 in 1966.

For export orders, the Znamya Truda factory built the MiG-21U in parallel with fighter versions during 1964–'68.

From the outset the trainer was dubbed *Sparka* (Twin). Despite its

low power, the MiG-21U speed and handling was similar to the single-seat. In 1965 one of the first was retrofitted with an up-rated engine and used to set women's records. On 22 May 1965 Natalya Prokhanova set a dynamic (zoom trajectory) height record at 24,336 m (79,843 ft). On 23 June Lydia Zaitseva held a sustained altitude of 19,020 m (62,402 ft). The aircraft was reported to the FAI as the Ye-33, never issued by MiG (apparently, some official chose to halve Ye-66!).

Bulgarian MiG-21US Red 05, retired and on show in a museum. (Russian Aviation Research Trust)

This MiG-21US is serving as a testbed for equipment trials. It is a single-seater with the rear cockpit carrying special test equipment. The rear cockpit also includes a puzzling blister and fairing on the right side of the fuselage. Trials are recorded by a camera on the fin. The wing pylon is of a deep MiG-23 type. (Yefim Gordon archive)

Snow-encrusted VVS MiG-21UM in three-tone camouflage. Note the callsign number "White 204" repeated on the vertical and ventral stabalizers. (Yefim Gordon)

An early MiG-21U was used to test the Czech design of ejection seat. The rear cockpit had an all-metal canopy with an open top. The black lines provided reference axes for cine film recording each test trajectory. (L+K)

During production of the MiG-21U, the nosewheel was changed to the disc-braked KT-102. Quite early in Tbilisi production, and later in Moscow, the trainers had the final (5.2 m^2 – 55.92 inches) broad vertical tail with the parabrake (often of the improved cruciform type) relocated below the rudder.

In 1966 the Tbilisi factory switched to making the upgraded MiG-21US, Type 68. As its designation implied, this was fitted with the RD-11F2S-300 engine and SPS blown flaps to train pilots in SPS operation. There was also a slight increase in internal fuel capacity to 2,450 liters (539 gallons) or 2,030 kg, the option of fitting four pylons, and the installation of a new crew-escape system. In the front cockpit the pupil had a KM-1U seat, while the instructor had a KM-1I, both being versions of the SK-3.

The pupil could not eject the instructor; the minimum usable speed was 130 km/h (80 mph).

In 1974, long after the later MiG-21UM was available, the Ye-6US development aircraft was fitted with an RD-11F2S-300 engine up-rated to 7 tonnes (15,432 lbs) thrust. It was used for women's time-to-height records. On 6 June Svetlana Savitskaya achieved times to 3, 6, 9, and 12 km (9,843, 19,685, 29,528, and 39,370

MiG-21US cockpits, front and rear. (Yefim Gordon)

ft) of 59.1 seconds, 1 minute 20.4 seconds; 1 minute 46.7 seconds; and 2 minutes 35.1 seconds. On 15 November she bettered these figures to, respectively, 41.2 seconds; 1 minute 0.1 seconds; 1 minute, 21 seconds; and 1 minute 59.3 seconds. On the second occasion the aircraft was fitted with "two TTRD of 2,300 kg," these being SPRD-99 assisted takeoff rockets, which were jettisoned on burnout.

Production of the MiG-21US took place only in Tbilisi, both for home and export customers, the total built being 347. In the course of production a periscope was added and linked to the gear select – something many instructors had requested from 1962. The final trainer version – the MiG-21UM, Type 69 – was again manufactured only at Tbilisi, which produced 1,133 in 1971–'75. This naturally incorporated all the previous upgrades plus an improved cockpit and avionics. Altogether the Sparka family proved both a com-

mercial and operational success. Every one of the 40-odd air forces that used the MiG-21 also used the trainer. As well as its basic duty of conversion to type, it proved excellent at teaching aerobatics up to and beyond Mach 1, blind flying at all speeds, and also simple air-to-air and air-to-ground weapon delivery. A number have also been used as test-beds, one Czech example being used to develop a Czech ejection seat, fired from the rear cockpit.

VARIATIONS ON A THEME

The MiG-21 was also used as the basis for five aircraft in three families whose purpose was wholly experimental. All were grossly modified, only bearing a superficial resemblance to the original MiG-21. Additionally there were various, less fundamental, research programs flown by otherwise standard MiG-21s. One of these was the testing of skis. It had always been important for Soviet landplanes to be cleared to operate from ice and compacted snow on skis. It is more difficult with supersonic jets because of higher takeoff and landing speeds, the need for directional stability and retractable skis. Extensive ski testing took place in 1960 using the Ye-5/2 prototype. Sadly, no photographs have yet been found – the tests took place from May to July.

The skis, of two types, were fitted to the main legs only, and did not retract. One design was almost rectangular with an upturned front. The other was circular with an upturned rim all round, because this pattern was free to rotate. The test program was entrusted to OKB pilot Igor M. Kravtsov, and skis were changed after each flight. The greatest difficulty was encountered in maintaining control while taxiing. The best answer was the KL, wheel/ski arrangement, used on the Su-7BKL. This used a steel ski hardly larger than the wheel, mounted on its own shock struts at a steep nose-up angle. KL landing gear can retract inside the normal wheel bay. None of these were put into production. In 1965 Kravtsov was killed in the MiG Ye-152A, a twin-engine delta unrelated to the MiG-21.

Another experimental program that did not lead to production was the redesigned air inlet. It was tested

An official portrait of Red 81, *the Ye-8/1. For its immature engine this could have led to the MiG-21 family taking a new direction with dramatically changed appearance. (RSK MiG)*

The Ye-8/1. Note the twin auxiliary inlet doors are open. (RSK MiG)

Three official views of the Ye-8/2, revealing numerous details of this potentially impressive aircraft. The Sapfir-21 radar was eventually to equip the MiG-21bis. (RSK MiG)

right at the end of the MiG-21 program by the Kiev VVS Institute. Throughout the history of the MiG-21, a basic shortcoming had been the tendency of the engine – no matter whether an RD-11, R-13, or R-25 – to misbehave whenever the inlet failed to travel exactly in the direction it was pointing.

Trials were made by the Kiev VVS Institute using a Type 75, MiG-21bis (75002198), originally manufactured in 1973. The radar was replaced by a ballast, and the inlet was fitted with a ring of inward-opening doors, each hinged at the front. These formed a complete ring round the nose, broken only by the PVD boom, to take care of any off-

design condition in either pitch or yaw. Inlet angle sensors supplied two control-system fairings along the upper side of the nose. It worked well, but was not adopted as a service retrofit.

Turning to the major experimental aircraft, the first of these chronologically was the Ye-8, following a Kremlin decree of 1961 for a new version capable of destroying hostile aircraft at night or in bad weather. It was to be the "MiG-23," a service designation that had been used before and was eventually used to identify a later and totally different aircraft. The radar was to be the RP-22, the Volkov Sapfir-21, and the engine the more powerful

R-21F. In the Ye-8 the bold decision was taken to redesign the nose to house the radar alone, and – with no wing spars crossing the fuselage – to curve the engine air duct down to a completely separate inlet under the forward fuselage. Later, in the Ye-7 prototypes, the task was accomplished with a reflector of reduced diameter.

The Tumanskii engine design team was led by N. Metskhvarishvili. Though based on the RD-11F, the engine had the compressor inlet diameter increased (from 772 mm to 845 mm, 33.27 in) to handle a considerably greater airflow. The afterburner was a new design, with a particularly efficient convergent/divergent multi-flap nozzle, giving exceptional augmentation. Unlike all other MiG-21 versions, this nozzle projected beyond the end of the fuselage. The R-21F was potentially an outstanding engine, but tragically its immaturity was to prove lethal to the aircraft program and almost to the life of its original OKB pilot.

The Ye-8 bristled with other modifications. The most obvious was the addition of a foreplane, called by the OKB a destabilizer. As previously tested on the Ye-6T/3, this comprised two cropped-delta surfaces, each with a long anti-flutter

It was traditional for the official LII photos to be taken with the nominated test pilot in the cockpit. In the case of the Ye-8/2 it was Fedotov. Note the folded ventral fin. (RSK MiG)

Looking down on the Ye-8/2, showing the nozzle of the R-21F-300 engine and the vertical tail resembling that of the Ye-7/8. (RSK MiG)

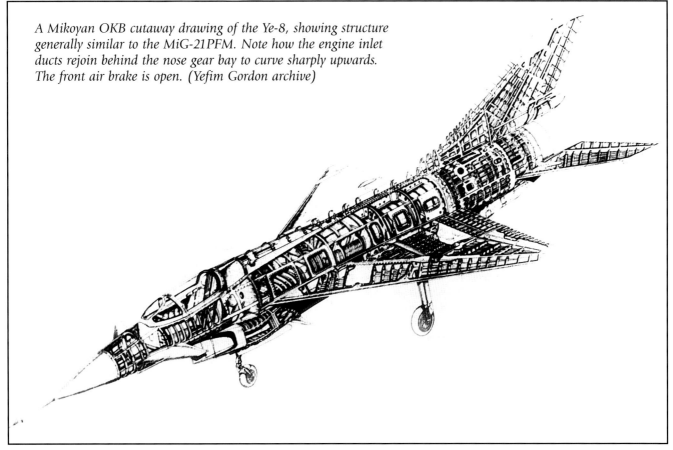

A Mikoyan OKB cutaway drawing of the Ye-8, showing structure generally similar to the MiG-21PFM. Note how the engine inlet ducts rejoin behind the nose gear bay to curve sharply upwards. The front air brake is open. (Yefim Gordon archive)

and balance mass halfway from root to tip. Its span was 2.6 m (102.4 in), mounted horizontally just below the fuselage centerline. In normal flight they pivoted freely to align with the local airflow. At over Mach 1 the air data system signaled a mechanical lock that held these surfaces aligned with the longitudinal axis. The switch from free to locked was imperceptible, the airflow always being close to the longitudinal axis at over Mach 1. Addition of these "destabilizers" increased the lift coefficient by a factor of 2 at Mach 2 and by more than twice at Mach 1.5. At Mach 2 at an altitude of 15 km (49,200 ft) the "destabilizers" enabled maximum sustained turn to be increased from 2.5g to 5.1g, leading to a dramatically superior fighter.

The tailplanes were taken directly off the production line, but were mounted 135 mm (5.3 in) lower than usual. The fin was of the intermediate size, as used on the Ye-6V and Ye-7; it was of the round-topped shape as on the Ye-7/8. To improve directional stability, the Ye-8 was fitted with an enlarged ventral fin. The available depth was extremely limited, so the fin hinged

Compared with the MiG-21PFM, on which it was based, the 23-31 had a longer fuselage with a bulged mid-section, fixed landing gear, and many other modifications. (Yefim Gordon archive)

The official side view of the 23-31, or Ye-7PD, showing the camera/theodolite target markings at nose and tail, the open lift bay door, and the cable fairing serving electrical equipment displaced from the spine to the nose. (Yefim Gordon archive)

The 23-31, sectioned and stripped and in use in the Moscow Aviation and Technological Institute. (Yefim Gordon archive)

sideways prior to landing. On selecting landing gear down, a hydraulic jack pulled the fin up to lie horizontally towards the right. This novel idea was repeated later with the official MiG-23.

Another major innovation was to use integral tanks throughout. This proved a great success, reducing weight and significantly increasing capacity. Nine compartments held a total of 3,200 liters (704 gallons), or about 2,655 kg. Integral tanks were a feature of all subsequent Mikoyan fighters except the MiG-25.

Wings were also taken off the production line, with SPS flaps, though with a slightly modified leading-edge structure. There was only one airbrake, squeezed in between the nose and main landing gears. The PVD-7 boom was rigidly mounted on the tip of the nose.

The landing gears differed in various respects. The nose unit retracted to the rear and was taller and stronger than the normal design. It also carried a larger disc-braked wheel and tire. The main units used large (Ye-7 type) wheels and tires, with an increased track of 2,787 mm (110 in). The wheelbase was dramatically reduced to only 3,350 mm (11 ft). This tended to make the Ye-8 nod when braking or taxiing over uneven ground.

The cockpit contained a KM-1 seat, and the canopy was unlike that of any other MiG-21, with a fixed forward section and a long main hood hinged to the right, with only a narrow metal frame at the rear. Behind it was a partly glass-fiber spine housing internal communications antennas. The parabrake was installed above the jet pipe.

Final design decisions were taken in June 1961, by which time Factory No.155 was engaged in building two Ye-8s. Ye-8/1 was ready at Zhukovskii on 5 March 1962. It initially had a metal nose

housing an inert mass in place of the radar, a wing with the original area-increasing slotted flaps (without blowing), no pylons, and a non-standard large-diameter parabrake housing. It began testing on 17 April 1962 in the hands of OKB chief test pilot Mosolov. From the fifth flight a succession of engine malfunctions were experienced, followed by compressor stalls and a flameout. On flight Nos. 21 and 25 the engine was changed to one with larger turbine stators. On flight 40 on 11 September 1962, about 60 km (37 miles) from Zhukovskii at Mach 1.7 at a height of 10 km, the sixth compressor stage disintegrated. Part of the disc destroyed the right aileron, causing very rapid roll, while sudden loss of thrust and flow reversal in the inlet duct caused violent deceleration. Mosolov was unable to regain control. He was injured ejecting inverted at an altitude of 8 km, and further injured on landing.

He was not found for 2-1/2 hours after the crash, but his life was saved.

The Ye-8/2 had no radar, but it had blown flaps, two pylons, auxiliary pitots on each side of the nose, and later a blade antenna on the spine. The assigned pilot was Aleksandr V. Fedotov, who made 13 reasonably trouble free flights between 29 June and 4 September 1962. Despite this, the loss of the Ye-8/1 and need for a reliable engine terminated the program. Most OKB engineers had regarded the Ye-8 as the fighter of the future, and regretted this decision.

In the early 1960s, the MiG bureau – increasingly called the AI Mikoyan OKB after the retirement of Guryevich in 1964 – was studying ways of reconciling the conflicting demands of high supersonic speed with the ability to disperse. The answer appeared to lie either in the use of dedicated lift turbojets, used only at takeoff and landing, or in a variable sweep wing which, when extended to maximum span, could deploy high-lift leading and trailing edge devices.

The OKB began to work in parallel on three totally different prototypes. The 23-01 was a completely new design of delta-winged aircraft, superficially resembling the MiG-21, but larger and with a very powerful main engine and two lift jets. The 23-11/1 was roughly the same size, but had a high-mounted variable sweep wing. The smaller 23-31 was built quickly in order to get flight

The 23-31 had quite a high minimum airspeed, and normally flew with partial flap and tailplanes at large positive incidence. It is seen here performing at the Domodyedovo airshow in July 1967. Note the telemetry antenna ahead of the nose landing gear. (Yefim Gordon archive)

An official portrait of the MiG-21I/1, painted pale grey and with the national flag and civil registration SSSR A-144 on the fin. (RSK MiG)

On its first flight on 31 December 1968 the first Tu-144, Article 44-00, was closely accompanied by its analog, the MiG-21I/1. (Yefim Gordon archive)

Official portrait of the MiG-21I/2, with fin-tip camera. Note the deep underwing powered flight control unit fairings. (RSK MiG)

experience with the lift-jet installation of the 23-01. At the outset it was felt that the 23-01 might go into production, with the VVS designation of "MiG-23." There was never any serious expectation of building the 23-31 in series.

After the first flight by Ostapenko on 16 June 1966 he commented: "For takeoff you need maximum dry power on the main engine, but for landing you need afterburner!" Subsequent flying was shared with B. A. Orlov. Both

pilots agreed that, while abundant thrust was available in all flight regimes, the aircraft was basically unstable at low airspeeds and control was inadequate.

The last of the pure research conversions were the two Type 21-11

aircraft was "Analog," because the purpose of the 21-11 was to assist in the design of the Tupolev Tu-144 Charger supersonic transport. The first aircraft, the 21-11/1, was built as a test vehicle to explore stability and control of the tailless configuration. The 21-11/2 was assigned the task of investigating the exact shape of wing that should be used on the Tu-144, with different types of LERX. To be of real use, both should have flown at least two years before completion of the first Tu-144.

Both were originally production MiG-21S fighters, rebuilt with little of the original wing left except the main spars, forward tanks and main gear bay. The 21-11/1 was completed with a graceful wing extending at the root almost from nose to tail. The inboard (forward) section had a constant leading-edge sweep of 78°, curving round to a constant 55° outboard, resulting in a broad tip. On the trailing edge were four fully powered surfaces, the inboard pair serving as un-blown flaps and the outer pair as elevons. The power units were housed in prominent under-wing fairings, those for the elevons occupying the entire chord of the wing. Thanks to the increased volume available in the wing, the internal fuel capacity was increased from 2,320 to 2,715 kg (3,270 liters, 719 gallons).

In a chicken-and-egg situation, Mikoyan could hardly finish the 21-11/1 until he knew the way the wing should be designed. The Tupolev OKB did not want to complete the Tu-144 prototype until data was in from testing not just the first Analog but the 21-11/2 as well. In 1968 A. N. Tupolev, who was then 80, lived in the same apartment block as Mikoyan. In the end, the whole program was far too late to have useful input to the Tu-144. The 21-11/1 at last began flying on 18 April 1968, in the hands of Oleg V. Gudkov. By this time the prototype Tu-144 was virtually complete,

The I/2 with the (original shape) right wing tufted, while the left wing is being rebuilt with a new root extension. Note camera targets at the nose and tail, and the badge of the Komsomolskiy Molodyozhnyy Ekipazh – KME, the "young man's crew". (LII archive)

aircraft, perhaps better known as the MiG-21I. One author has stated that this stood for *Issledovaniye* (research), but in fact it stood for

Imitator. (This was the first use of the "I" suffix, later to be used on the MiG-21-93.) Another (unofficial) name for the wing research

Analog, or Imitator, the MiG-21I experimental was designed to pave the way for the so-called "Concordski," the Tupolev Tu-144 supersonic airliner. The survivor of two is displayed at Monino. (Yefim Gordon archive)

Side by side at Monino are the MiG-21I Analog and the Tupolev Tu-144 Charger. In the end, the former was unable to provide much in the way of advanced information for the latter. (Yefim Gordon archive)

the 21-11/1 acted as chase aircraft on its first flight from Zhukovskii on 31 December 1968.

The 21-11/1 was fully painted and bore civil registration SSSR-1966, which was originally the planned date of its first flight. It was flown intensively, with the cg position varied. Very soon it had taken the flight envelope to 19 km (62,340 ft) over a speed range from 212 km/h to Mach 2.06. It was flown by Tu-144 test pilots Eduard Yelyan and Mikhail Kozlov, each making four flights. Later it was used to convert several other pilots. LII pilot I. Volk first flew the 21-11/2 in late 1969. This was fitted with a succession of different LERXs. In addition to the usual flight test instrumentation, the starboard (right hand) wing was completely tufted and a cine camera was mounted on top of the fin to photograph the tufts. A second camera was later added, looking over the wing from just behind the canopy. The modified root sections increased wing area to about 43 m² (462 ft²). This aircraft also differed in that all four trailing edge surfaces were elevons, each capable of providing control in either pitch or roll.

By the end of 1969, the two aircraft had made 140 test or conversion flights in the hands of 11 pilots. The lead pilots, Gudkov and Volk, greatly enjoyed flying these aircraft. They even suggested to Mikoyan that he should build a fighter version. They pointed out that, compared with the series MiG-21 fighters, the tailless machines had much greater wing area and, in most respects, even better maneuverability. The take-off, landing, and rate of roll were particularly good. Agility at high altitudes was also significantly enhanced.

The 21-11/2 continued to fly useful research programs for several years, and was finally retired to the VVS Museum at Monino. Unfortunately, the 21-11/1 was destroyed on 28 July 1970. LII pilot Viktor Konstantinov carried out his first conversion flight and then returned to Zhukovskii. Presumably elated at the handling of the aircraft, he proceeded to carry out unauthorized aerobatics at low level. These included upward rolls, with elevon deflections seen from the ground to be near the limit. He lost control when inverted and was killed.

MADE IN CHINA

After using almost 2,000 MiG-15 fighters over Korea, the People's Republic of China turned to the MiG OKB to acquire self-sufficiency in military aircraft. In 1955 a manufacturing license was obtained for the MiG-17F with 767 built. In 1965 the Chengdu factory developed a two-seat trainer version, the JJ-5 (Jianjiji-Jiaolianji, fighter trainer), and made over 1,200. In 1960 the cultural break interrupted license-production of the MiG-19, but with painstaking skill the Shenyang engineers "reverse engineered" a pattern aircraft and put it into production as the J-6. They also developed a trainer version, the JJ-6. This was quite different from the MiG counterpart, which was only produced as a prototype.

In 1961, a license was obtained for the MiG-21F-13 and its RD-11F-300 engine, and it fell to the Shenyang plant to initiate production in China. With cooperation with the Soviet Chief Administration of Aviation Industry (GUAP), several pattern aircraft and CKD kits were delivered for assembly. By accident or design, the supporting technical documentation is alleged to have been inadequate. The Chinese took time to build this aircraft, designation J-7, and its engine became the WP-7 (*Wopen*, engine jet). With the support of the Shenyang complex, it had been hoped that the Chengdu factory could, by 1964, produce the J-7 using engines from the Guizhou factory. However, the program was delayed by the Cultural Revolution.

In 1964 a single J-7 was being slowly assembled at Shenyang using some Chinese-made components. The first WP-7 engine first ran at Shenyang in October 1965. It was rated at the same thrusts as the Soviet RD-11F-300, and initially had a time between overhauls (TBO) of only 100 hours. Static testing of the first J-7 prototype was completed in November 1965 and this aircraft flew for the first time on 17 January 1966. By June 1967, limited production of the J-7I, the initial series version for the People's Liberation Army Air Force (PLAAF), had started at Chengdu.

The J-7I was almost identical to the MiG-21F-13. It had a single copy of the NR-30 gun, and was eventually fitted with two underwing pylons. Only a modest number were built because of dissatisfaction with the escape system, though batches were sold to Albania and Tanzania with the designation F-7A. In price, these undercut the corresponding Soviet product, which was no longer in production.

Progress during the Cultural Revolution continued to be slow. While aware of developments by the MiG OKB, the Chinese plants were unable to implement even the more obvious upgrades and almost

The J-7 prototype (MiG-21F-13) was produced by the Shenyang Aircraft Group Industry Corporation Ltd. and was first flight-tested by the test pilot Ge Wenyong on 17 January 1966. The domestic J-7 aircraft started to equip for the services in March 1967. The production was transferred to the Chengdu Aircraft Industrial Corporation in August 1968. (China Aircraft)

This J-7I is stored in the Datanchang Aviation Museum near Beijing. The main difference between J-7I and the prototype is that the drag parachute stowage at the tail has shifted up to the root of the vertical fin. The J-7I was produced by the Chengdu Aircraft Industrial Corporation. (Yefim Gordon archive)

A typical Chinese propaganda picture of J-7I fighters of the People's Liberation Army Air Force. Note the hinged arm over the seat, adjusted for pilot height, which is pushed down by the canopy. (Yefim Gordon archive)

The J-7II (export version F-7II) is an upgrade version based on the F-7I. The main upgrade items are: the forward-hinging canopy is changed to the fold-back canopy; the aircraft drag chute is shifted up to improve the aircraft landing performance and reduce landing distance; the 720-liter fuselage auxiliary tank is employed to increase the flight range and endurance time; the WP-7B engine is retrofitted to increase thrust and improve the aircraft performance. (China Aircraft)

all the development effort was applied to two derived projects. One was the J-8, a larger twinjet based on MiG-21 aerodynamics. The prototype flew on 5 July 1969, and though further design work was prohibited, flight-testing was permitted to continue. Development got underway after the Cultural Revolution in 1976, and a production prototype J-8 flew on 24 April 1978. A few J-8 fighters were built in 1984–'87, with simple ranging radar for two NR-30 guns and four under-wing PL-2B AAMs distantly derived from the Sidewinder. The ASCC assigned this aircraft the reporting name Finback, suffix letters being added for subsequent versions.

Surviving J-8s were brought up to the standard of the J-8I, which was produced in 1986–'90. This was fitted with the Sichuan SR-4 radar, very similar to the Soviet RP-22, and with a Type 23-3 twin-barrel gun (based on the GSh-23L) scabbed underneath immediately behind the nose gear. This eventually led to the visibly different J-8II dual-role fighter/attack version. A powerful monopulse radar with a large antenna was fitted into the redesigned nose. Various shore-based naval and export versions with digital Western avionics have continued in advanced development.

The other spin-off proved to be a dead end. Launched in 1969, the Nanchang J-12 was a short takeoff and landing (STOL) light fighter with a slatted swept wing. It was powered by a single LM (Shenyang) WP-6Z engine derived from the RD-9 used in the earliest MiG-21 prototypes. Though quite an attractive little machine, it was discontinued after many alterations in 1977.

Continued on page 73

THE MiG-21 IN COLOR

The Ye-2 prototype was the first swept wing prototype. It made its first flight on 14 February 1955 with MiG OKB test pilot G. K. Mossolov at the controls. The next prototype, Ye-2A, had a large wing fence on top of each wing. (RSK MiG)

While black and white photographs of most of the MiG-21 prototypes have been in print before, color from the same era is very rare. The large wing fences and a look at the shadow reveal this to be the swept-wing Ye-2A. (RSK MiG)

The Ye-4/2 prototype featured three wing fences extending back from the leading edge of the wing. The tube extending upward between the first and second wing fence was a visual indicator that the main landing gear was down and locked. (RSK MiG)

The Ye-5 prototype differed from the Ye-4 in the engine installed. The Ye-5 was powered by 5,098 lb-st AM-11 power plant, which boosted the top speed by nearly 700 kph (434.9 mph). The Ye-5 was unveiled on 24 June 1955 and NATO assigned the reporting name Fishbed to the prototype. (RSK MiG)

The Ye-6U/1, first of the two-seaters. (RSK MiG)

Red 82, the second Ye-8 with almost certainly Fedotov in the cockpit. (RSK MiG)

MiG-21SM with UB-16-57 rocket pods. (Yefim Gordon archive)

A MiG-21UM parked on what would be called pierced-steel plating (PSP) in the West, at Akhtyubinsk in June 1995. The eagle motif is worn by several NII-VVS aircraft. (Yefim Gordon)

A view of an experimental MiG-21 version. The aircraft was involved in the testing of a new or improved radar. Note the cable fairing, which is carrying trunking from the radar, rearwards over the callsign Red 44 *on the nose. (Yefim Gordon)*

MiG-21PFM 6613 Red *of the Polskie Wojska Lotnicze. (Waclaw Holys)*

German Luftwaffe MiG-21MF in "celebratory" colors for the wind-down of JG-1's MiGs. Not only has the nose received "shark's mouth" treatment, but the wing drop tanks have a more accurate shark eyes, teeth, and gills! (Yefim Gordon archive)

MiG-21bis 9483 Red *of the Polskie Wojska Lotnicze. (Waclaw Holys)*

Slovakian MiG-21MF 7714 Black. (Russian Aviation Research Trust)

Air-to-air of another specially painted Czech example, in this case MiG-21MF 7711 Black. (Russian Aviation Research Trust)

502 white, Bulgarian Air Force MiG-21bis in its natural habitat of a shelter embankment at Graf Ignatievo in 2002. (Peter Davison)

The distinctive bulge below the cockpit denotes an Egyptian MiG-21RF, in this case serial number "8502." (Russian Aviation Research Trust)

68

MiG-21MF 224 Blue (with SIAI-Marchetti SF.260WS Warrior behind) derelict at Mogadishu, Somalia. The crude painting on the nose presum-ably stands for "Air Force Explosive Ordnance Disposal." (Paul A Jackson)

Cambodian MiG-21UM 7114 Red taken post-1989, apparently out-of-use. Cambodian machines are currently undergoing an upgrade programme with IAI Lahav. (A J Walg – Aero Mapho)

MiG-21U-400 two seater 1216 awaiting its turn outside the Elbit upgrade facility in Bacau, Romania seen on a visit in 1998. (Peter Davison)

A fully upgraded MiG-21MF Lancer C at the Royal International Air Tattoo, Fairford, Gloucestershire in 2005; one of a flight of four that visited the United Kingdom that summer. (Peter Davison)

A former East German Air Force MiG-21PFM in Luftwaffe colors. (Marcus Fulber)

The Museo dell'Aviazione, on the border of the Republic of San Marino contains this MiG-21PFM in Iranian Air Force colors. It was originally an East German aircraft ironically destined for sale to Iraq. (Peter Davison)

Mongolian pilots talk tactics in front of a camouflaged MiG-21PFM 009 White. (Mongolian Air Force)

MG-114, a Finnish Air Force MiG-21bis, taxies out for another mission. (Jyrki Laukkanen)

Soviet AF MiG-21 PFM nose section, canopy open. (Yefim Gordon)

A Czech Air Force MiG-21UM Mongol B, Black 9341, parked on the ramp of its home base. (Martin Novak)

The Chinese J-7 è fighters equipped for the PLAAF are shown. (Yefim Gordon archive)

With the disbandment of the Warsaw Pact, the Hungarian Air Force changed its national markings several times. The markings finally adopted were nearly the same as their World War II markings, a chevron in red, white, and green. This MiG-21UM, Red 3041, carries a non-standard three-tone camouflage. (Yefim Gordon archive)

The export F-7 IIA fighter was produced by the Chengdu Aircraft Industrial Corporation. (Yefim Gordon archive)

The FT-7 is an advanced jet trainer developed by the Guizhou Aircraft Industrial Corporation on the basis of the F7II. It can perform all train programs of the F-7, F-7I, and F-7II, and most training programs of F-7III and F-8 family. It also has certain ground-attack capability. (Chinese Military Aviation)

The low-altitude and takeoff/landing performance of the F-7E used by the "August 1" Aerobatic Flying Team for flight presentation are improved because the double-delta wing and leading edge maneuver flap are employed. (via Yefim Gordon)

Cockpit of a MiG-21U. The fuselage was redesigned to accommodate the pupil in the front cockpit and the instructor in an added rear cockpit. SK seats were standard. In front of the pupil was a fixed windshield with a near oval flat front screen. (Waclaw Holys)

After 1976 the Chengdu factory, supported by Shenyang, was able to press ahead with the long-planned J-7II, flying the first example on 30 December 1978. This introduced a Chengdu copy of the SK seat, called Type II, which was hinged upwards at the rear and matched with a fixed-windscreen unit. Other modifications included the WP-7B engine with TBO doubled to 200 hours, parabrake relocated under the rudder, three pylons with the centerline plumbed for a 720-liter (158.4-gallon) tank, and a new Lanzhou compass system.

Normally two 30-mm guns are installed. In Chinese service, the PL-2 or PL-7 missiles can be carried, while the F-7B export version – supplied to Egypt and Iraq from 1982 – can be matched with the French Matra R.550 Magic AAM. In 1991 Sri Lanka became the first user of the F-7BS with four wing pylons.

Many observers were astonished that the People's Republic could continue to sell fighters that belong to a bygone age. After considering various alternatives, the Chinese Ministry of Aero-Space Industry decided in the late 1970s on a two-pronged approach to keep the local products competitive. One was to emulate the MiG OKB in developing a fighter called J-7III in 1981, resembling the MiG-21MF/Type 96F. The other, which was generally preferred, was to keep the basic aircraft but upgrade it in

J-7 II fighters equipped for the Chinese naval air force. (Yefim Gordon archive)

The J-7II (F-7II) employs the delta wing as its plane shape. In comparison with the F-6, it has merits of high speed, high ceiling, and flexible handling and is highly praised by the Air Force and Navy. (China Aircraft)

The J-7III all-weather fighter was first flown successfully by Yu Mingwen on 26 April 1984. (Yefim Gordon archive)

The J-7III's fuselage is thicker and longer than other J-7s. There is a dorsal fin on the fuselage and a 23 mm two-barrel gun under the central belly. A rear view mirror is added at the top of the canopy. (China Aircraft)

A line of PLAAF J-III fighters. (Yefim Gordon archive)

detail and fit a new avionics suite. Some items were imported as early as May 1979, but actual development of the upgraded F-7M began in parallel with the J-7III in 1981. In 1986 this version was given the name Airguard.

The basic Airguard still retains the original 690-mm nose inlet, precluding installation of search radar, as well as the 4.08 m² (43.9 ft²) fin as fitted to the later MiG-21F-13, and a similar fuel system, with capacity reduced from 2,470 to 2,385 liters (524.5 gallons). Surprisingly, the main tires have a diameter of only 600 mm (23.62 in), and inflation pressure of 1.15 MPa (166.8 psi), limiting operations to paved runways. Modifications include a four-pylon wing. The seat is the CAC zero-height pattern, based on the SK. The air data boom has been moved to starboard, above the nose, and is no longer pivoted. The tailplane anti-flutter masses are shorter and less pointed. The most welcome improvement to the WP-7B(BM) engine was eliminating the need for a separate starting fuel tank and supply system using gasoline. Total

engine weight was reduced, and 40 afterburner firings are permitted in each 200-hour period.

Though still equipped solely with traditional electro-mechanical dial instruments, the Airguard cockpit was completely updated. At top center is the heads-up display and weapon-aiming computer (HUDWAC), which is the GEC-Ma coni Type 956. The same company supplied the AD.3400 two-band UHF/VHF multi-function communications radio, with high security measures. Other new avionics items included GMAv Type 226 Skyranger target-ranging radar, incorporating new electronic counter-measures (ECCM), angle-of-attack sensor on the port side of the nose, an air-data computer, WL-7 radio compass, XS-6A marker beacon receiver, Type 602 IFF transponder, and Type 0101 HR-A/2 radar altimeter. Some of these were derived from Soviet designs. To match the improved avionics, the electrical system required upgrading – three static examples replaced four rotary inverters. The Jianghuai YX-3 gaseous oxygen system is also fitted.

The standard Airguard was fitted with two Type 30-1 guns, each with 60 rounds. The four wing pylons can accommodate PL-2, -2A, -2B, -5, or -7, or Magic AAMs, or either the 18 x 57 mm or 7 x 90 mm rocket launchers, or bombs up to the 500 kg (1,102 lbs) type. The centerline pylon can carry a 500 or 800 liter (110 or 176 gallon) tank, and the outer wing pylons the 500-liter size.

After several years, the F-7M Airguard was publicly revealed in October 1984. Important orders were soon placed by Egypt, Iran, Bangladesh, Myanmar (formerly Burma), and Zimbabwe. The Pakistan Air Force (PAF) ordered a variant designated F-7P, which was briefly given the name Skybolt. This incorporated 24 modifications, the most important of which were Martin-Baker Mk.10L seats with zero-height, zero-airspeed capability, and the ability to fire

four Sidewinder AAMs. The latest PAF variant is the F-7MP, delivered in 1994–'95. This has a new navigation and fire-control system, and an improved cockpit layout. In 1989 Rockwell Collins in the USA delivered 100 sets of new avionics, including the ARN-147 VOR/ILS receiver, ARN-149 ADF, and Pro-Line II digital DME-42. FIAR in Italy supplied Grifo fire-control radars, which fit inside the original small nose cone. All these items are fitted to the F-7MP, and will also be used to update the existing F-7P force.

In October 1982, the Chinese launched a version of the MiG-21US dual-control trainer built by the Guizhou Aviation Industry Corporation (GAIC), already participating in the production of the single-seats. Naturally called the JJ-7 (FT-7 denoting the export version), this was basically a clone of the Soviet MiG-21US. It incorporated a periscope for the instructor, as on the MiG-21UM, as well as changes introduced by the F-7M Airguard, apart from absence of the AoA sensor. The engine is the WP-7B(BM), and fuel capacity is slightly greater

After 1979, at the same time as the Chengdu Aircraft Industrial Corporation organized series production of the J-7 upgrade version, the company upgraded the J-7 (F-7) according to the requirements of foreign customers. The most successful upgrade version is the F-7M. The aircraft was first flown successfully by Yu Mingwen, Vice Leader of the Test Flight Regiment stationed at the company. (Yefim Gordon archive)

The F-7MG employs a newly designed double-delta wing with leading-edge and trailing-edge maneuver flaps, an engine with increased thrust, advanced avionics equipment and modern cockpit configuration. It has night-combat capability. The integrated close-range combat effectiveness of the F-7MG is 83.9% higher than that of the original J-7/F-7 family. (China Aircraft)

The F-7MG is one of the latest versions in the J-7/F-7 family. Its main feature is using the double-delta wing design with medium aspect ratio. The sweep angle of the leading edge of the inner wing is 57°, and that of the outer wing is 42°. It is shown that the leading edge flap is installed at the outboard wing (deflected down). There are two stored mounting points under each side of the wing, making weapon suspension more flexible. (Yefim Gordon archive)

The main differences between the F-7IIA and J-7I: the engine with higher thrust is retrofitted, the drag chute stowage is shifted up to the root of the vertical fin, and partial avionics equipment are retrofitted. (Yefim Gordon archive)

The F-7P aircraft was an export version produced by the Chengdu Aircraft Industrial Corporation. It was an upgrade version based on the F-7M. The aircraft could be used in the operation in daytime and under adverse weather conditions. (China Aircraft)

than for the F-7M at 2440 liters (536.7 gallons) and there is provision for three pylons for a maximum external load of 1,187 kg (2,617 lbs), maximum external fuel being 558 kg (1,230 lbs). A packaged Type 23-3 twin-barrel gun can be mounted on the centerline, aimed by an HK-03E optical sight.

The PAF trainer is the FT-7P. This has no instructor periscope, but has two pylons on each wing, an improved fire-control system incorporating the HUDWAC, and other cockpit improvements includ-

ing the air-data computer. Increased fuel capacity gives 25 percent greater range.

After four years of development, the prototype J-7III made its first flight on 26 April 1984. This was almost a clone of the MiG-21MF. However, most of the equipment was Chinese and not a direct copy. For example, the engine is the WP-13, which was developed in China jointly by Chengdu Engine Co and LMC, and is in production by the latter. Bleed air from the WP-13 supplies the blown flaps. The air

inlet was enlarged to accommodate a J-band radar designated JL-7. The broad 5.2 m^2 (56 ft^2) fin was fitted, and other changes included increased spine fuel and a Beijing Aeronautical Instruments KJ-11 two-channel (pitch and roll) autopilot, an HTY-4 "low-speed zero-height" seat, and a canopy hinged to the right incorporating a rear view periscope.

Avionics include the AoA sensor, an LJ-2 omni-directional RWR with its two aft-hemisphere passive antennas mounted on each side of

Two photographs of the F-7PG export fighter. (Chinese Military Aviation)

nated this collaboration, but CATIC continued studies with the Pakistan Aeronautical Complex. Preliminary design and tunnel testing has been completed. After buying over 100 F-7Ps in the 1980s and 90s, Pakistan ordered 66 F-7PGs, including nine FT-7PGs trainers, in 2002.

The modifications amounted to a total redesign. The wing is tapered on the leading edge so that though span is increased to 8.98 m (29 ft 5-1/2 in), the area increases only slightly to about 24.62 m² (265 ft²). The new leading edge begins with a highly swept root extension and is fitted with slats over the main portion. The tips carry missile launch rails. The capacious nose houses a powerful multi-mode radar. Variable side inlets supply air to a completely different engine that several observers have predicted will be a

the parabrake container (a feature not seen on any MiG-21), a GT-4 ECM jammer, Type 605A IFF (a copy of SRO-2), and an FJ-1 flight data recorder. The J-7 III was developed jointly by CAC and GAIC, and by 1993 was in service with the PLAAF. The F-7 III is a further upgraded version, reported to be in service with both the PLAAF and Navy.

In 1987 CAC, the PAF and Grumman Corporation of the USA (now Northrop Grumman) carried out a study of a major J-7 redesign called Sabre 2, using an American engine and avionics. This led to a formal agreement on 21 October 1988 between the China National Aero-Technology Import and Export Corporation (CATIC) and Grumman for an aircraft called CAC Super-7. In 1989, for political reasons, the U.S. Government termi-

Three official photos of a JJ-7 (FT-7) trainer. (CATIC/Chinese Military Aviation)

The FT-7P prototype made the maiden flight successfully on 9 November 1990. (Chinese Military Aviation)

A model of the Super-7, which since the departure of Grumman in 1989, has faded as an active project. (Paul A. Jackson)

The famous "August 1" Aerobatic Flying Team changed to fly the F-7E aircraft in 1997. (Yefim Gordon archive)

Klimov RD-33, as used in the twin-engine MiG-29.

Other features include a redesigned fuel system, with optimized spine capacity and single-point pressure fuelling, a new nose gear with power steering, upgraded main gears, a modified ventral fin, arrester hook, an updated cockpit with an advanced HUD, comprehensive avionics with a revised cooling system. The two Type 30-1 guns are replaced by an internal Type 23-3. Maximum takeoff weight is predicted to be 11,295 kg (24,900 lbs).

Another derivative of the basic J-7 is the J-7E. The J-7E incorporates wing features of the Super-7, the new outer panels (starting at the flap/aileron junction) having a leading-edge sweep of only 42°. These outer wings taper slightly on the trailing edge, so that wing area increases less than 2 m², even though span is increased to 8.32 m (27 ft 3-1/2 in). This wing has four pylon stations, the outers plumbed for 480-liter (105-gallon) tanks, and room for PL-8 AAMs. The engine is the WP-7F, with dry thrust considerably increased to 4.5 tons (9,921 lbs); rating with maximum afterburner is 6.5 tons (14,330 lbs). The J-7E is stressed for 8g up to Mach 0.8, and to 6.5g above this speed. Equipment includes digital avionics with a HUD and air data computer.

MIKOYAN GUREVICH
MiG-21 FISHBED

79

The MiG-21 engaged many enemies in three big conflicts and countless small ones. The big conflicts were the Indo-Pakistan wars, the Yom Kippur War between Israel and several Arab countries, and the Vietnam War. The MiG-21 versions that fought in these conflicts were mainly of the PF/PFM type, plus a smaller number of MF/FL.

The MiG-21 achieved significant success over India and Vietnam, but fared less well in the Middle East where the opposition was mainly the Mirage IIICJ. It was only inferior in radar, flight endurance, and cockpit field of view. There was also a disparity between the combat training, experience, and aggressive spirit of the Israeli pilots. Nevertheless, the results were distressing to the MiG OKB.

The MiG-21 could have seen action over Cuba, during the missile crisis of 1962–'63. A photograph of Camilo Cienfuegos airfield at Santa Clara on 10 November 1962 showed Fishbeds with missiles under their wings, and the Soviet fighters – MiG-21F-13s – soon appeared at other locations. Had Fidel Castro and Nikita Khrushchyev not backed down, there is little doubt that these aircraft would have taken on U.S. forces.

The first true war for the MiG-21 lasted 22 days in September 1965, between India and Pakistan. Here the main opponents were the F-86F and Hawker Hunter, though the Pakistan Air Force (PAF) had a handful of F-104As to pit against the Indian Air Force's still quite new MiG-21F-13s. Only eight MiGs could be fielded at the start, flying intensive combat air patrol (CAP) missions over the Punjab. Thus, results were inconclusive, though the IAF learned a great deal.

Every MiG-21F-13 Type 74 supplied to the Indian Air Force was Soviet-made by the Znamya Truda plant. (Russian Aviation Research Trust)

Servicing an Indian Air Force Type 77. (Yefim Gordon archive)

Three Type 77 MiG-21FL interceptors and two Type 66-400 trainers of the Indian Air Force. SRO-2 IFF is not fitted. (Russian Aviation Research Trust)

MiG-21PF-V interceptors during the Vietnam war. (Yefim Gordon archive)

These lessons were put to use when war against Pakistan resumed between 3 and 17 December 1971. MiG-21s, mainly of the FL type flown by IAF Nos.1, 4, 8, 28, 29, 30, 45, and 47 Squadrons, made numerous deep penetrations into West Pakistan but seldom encoun-tered the enemy. However, on the morning of 6 December, Flt Lt S. V. Shah, escorting HAL HF-24 Maruts on ground-attack sorties in the Sind-Rajasthan sector, destroyed a ground-hugging PAF Chinese-built F-6, opening fire with the GP-9 gun pod from long range (about 600 m, 2,000 ft) at a steep angle. Ironically, the MiG-21's first combat victory was against another MiG.

By 1971 few PAF F-104 Starfight-ers were still operational, but on the night of 4/5 December, 10 Starfight-ers of the Royal Jordanian Air Force flew to Masrur, Karachi, to come temporarily under PAF command. It was two of these aircraft that, on 12 December, began strafing targets on the south coast of the Rann (Gulf) of Kutch. Flt Lts Soni and Saigal were scrambled from Jamnagar and intercepted.

One F-104 escaped, but Soni was easily able to follow the other round in almost a 360° turn in full afterburner, at very low level. With speed rising beyond 1,200 km/h (about Mach 1), Soni closed on his target. At 900 m an F-104 in after-burner provides a good Sidewinder target, yet Soni selected guns. Amazingly, he hit, and the F-104 flamed. The pilot ejected and was reportedly captured.

This was hardly a combat, but a lucky strike on a fleeing opponent. However, on the last day of the war, 17 December, 29 (Black Scorpions) Squadron claimed four F-104s with-out loss. Operating from Uttarslai, Sqn Ldr I S Bindra, the CO, took off to escort Maruts when he was advised of a lone F-104 approaching at high speed. Bindra had no difficulty in get-ting on the tail of the F-104 and fired a K-13A missile, but this failed to achieve lock-on. He fired his other missile, and this exploded near the F-104's cockpit. Bindra then opened fire with 23 mm cannon, and the tar-get plunged into sandhills.

This delayed the Marut strike. Flt Lts N. Kukreya and A. Datta were flying escort when, approach-ing Umarkot, Kukreya said, "Two bogeys ahead!" One of the hostiles launched an AAM (undoubtedly a Sidewinder), which missed. Within seconds a stern chase developed, at about 500 m (1,600 ft), comprising the No. 2 F-104, Kukreya, the No. 1 F-104 (the AAM firer), and Datta. Datta advised Kukreya to turn hard to starboard, then found he was rapidly overtaking the F-104 in front, and that he was within K-13A firing parameters, as indicated by the headset audio note and the radar display. He fired both missiles and then switched to guns. Before he could take aim, the target erupt-ed in a fireball.

Kukreya broke to starboard as advised, but felt a judder ripple through his MiG. Afterwards it was surmised this may have been an

A Type 94 MiG-21PFM takes off in Vietnam. (Yefim Gordon archive)

This MiG-21PF-V interceptor (Red 5020) bears 12 kill markings (Russian Aviation Research Trust)

This MiG-21PF 807 of the Egyptian Air Force is in three-colour camouflage. It has the modified nozzle and parabrake installation. (Russian Aviation Research Trust)

engine surge caused by flying through air disturbed by gunfire from the F-104 behind, which was destroyed seconds later by Datta. Kukreya found that in full reheat he was also overhauling his target. The latter turned to port, and Kukreya found he could cut off the corner and close from 5-km range to 2 km (3 to 1.2 miles). He fired a K-13A, which failed. After about five seconds he fired the other, and this was detonated beside the target by its proximity fuse. Smoking, the F-104 spiraled down to the ground. The MiGs rejoined the Maruts, after an action lasting less than two minutes.

On the Eastern Front the MiG-21FL operated in both air superiority and ground-attack roles. Weapons were the K-13A, GP-9, FAB-500M62 bomb of 500 kg (1,102 lbs), napalm, UB-16-57 rocket launcher, and the S-24 rocket

of 240 mm caliber, which could be launched beyond the range of light AA fire. On the first attack mission, two aircraft equipped with guns and K-13As escorted four each armed with 500-kg bombs, which made deep craters in the runways of Tejagon air base near Dhaka (Dacca). Many hundreds of 57-mm rockets were fired. The U.S. magazine *Newsweek* recorded that A. A. Malik, Governor of East Pakistan (today Bangladesh), was "in a state of shock" and shakily wrote his notice of resignation, after salvoes of these missiles hit his residence.

Following this war, both Pakistan and India predictably expressed satisfaction with their aircraft. The MiG-21 could always out-turn the F-104 and also accelerate faster and overhaul it. It was the older F-86 and F-6 (MiG-19SF) that proved harder to beat, and on one occasion an F-86 shot down a MiG-21. According to the IAF, they ended the conflict with 45 losses and shot down 94 PAF aircraft in air combat. One aircraft, hit by AA fire, returned with three large areas of damage, strikes having removed fuselage skin over a region 1.22 x 0.33 m (48 x 13 in).

Turning to the Middle East, on 16 August 1966 an Iraqi pilot defected to Israel with his MiG-21F-13. Its new owners changed its true number of 534 for the James Bond 007, and it was extensively tested in Israel and the USA. In the Six-Day War of 5 through 10 June 1967 the decisive moment was the IDF/AF's

Egyptian MiG-21RF aircraft carried their optical cameras internally under the cockpit, requiring a shallow fairing behind the nosewheel. This example is serial number 8506. (via Russian Aviation Research Trust)

MiG-21MF "8611" of the Egyptian Air Force. (via Russian Aviation Research Trust)

Remarkable combat cine frame taken by an Israeli Mirage IIICJ showing strikes on an Egyptian MiG-21MF despite the 90° deflection shot. (Yefim Gordon archive)

initial pre-emptive strike on Arab air power. In about three hours some 300 United Arab Republic aircraft were destroyed, almost all on the ground. Few Egyptian or Syrian aircraft managed to get airborne, and only 19 Israeli aircraft were lost.

At least one MiG-21 was still serviceable on 7 June, because on that day an Iraqi example managed to score a hit with a K-13A missile on an Israeli Mirage. Shortly after the end of the Six-Day War, on 15 July 1967, the Israeli-developed Shafrir I AAM scored its first victory, downing an Egyptian MiG-21 from a range of 1.2 km (just under 4,000 ft). This missile was then developed into the much more reliable and very lethal Shafrir 2, which opened its scorebook on 22 July 1969, the loser again being an Egyptian MiG-21. By the time a full-scale war resumed, in October 1973, the Shafrir 2 had claimed 13 kills.

The UAR planned their war of revenge for 14:05 hours (2:05 PM) on 6 October 1973, the special holy day in the Jewish calendar called Yom Kippur. The initial assault was mounted against the three biggest IDF/AF bases by 222 Egyptian aircraft, of which over 100 were MiG 21s. It went well, but knocked out only a fraction of the Israeli air power. Things then got harder, and from the following day the MiG-21s flew top cover. On 14 October about 70 MiG-21s met a similar number of Israeli McDonnell F-4E Phantoms, the result was an 18-4 victory for the Egyptians. However, in 1977–'82 a carefully confirmed total of nearly 100 Syrian aircraft (the bulk being MiG-21s) were shot down in air combat by the IDF/AF without a single loss.

In contrast, fighting between Egypt and Libya in late July 1977 came out roughly even, though again what really happened is hard to discern. For example, while Egypt admitted losing just two Su-20s, Libya claimed 25 victories including seven MiG-21s.

Upwards of 100 MiG-21s found their last resting place in the former Portuguese colony of Angola. At first the F-13 and PF versions had little opposition, but throughout the 1980s MFs flown mainly by Cuban pilots were opposed by the

The unmistakable profile of a MiG-21 caught in the graticules of a HUD weapons sight. While this was often the case, there must be thousands of times when the graticules belonged to a MiG-21 and the outline to another type! (via Russian Aviation Research Trust)

União Nacional para a Independência Total de Angola (UNITA) and Frente Nacional de Libertação de Angola (FNLA) opposition parties, as well as by the South African Air Force in Namibia (former South West Africa).

A number of Soviet MiG-21 units were detached to Afghanistan from 1979 but saw only limited action and proved basically unsuited to that kind of guerrilla conflict. By contrast, Iraqi MiG-21s of several species more than held their own in numerous air combats against F-4s

Arab air force MiG-21s did not fare well against the Israelis. An early coup was the defection of an Iraqi example on 16 August 1966. This was evaluated by the IDF/AF who could not resist the "007" spy-type callsign and almost certainly went on to fly in the skies over Nellis Air Force Base, Nevada. The aircraft was photographed in the IDF/AF museum. (Yefim Gordon archive)

and F-5s of the Iranian Air Force. It was the opinion of the Iraqi pilots that, despite costing less than half as much as an F-4E, the F-5 was their most dangerous opponent.

Another region that has known little peace for over 20 years is the Horn of Africa, where the principal combatants have been Somalia and Ethiopia. In July through August 1977 a succession of air battles took place in which the main aircraft involved were Somali MiG-21MFs and Ethiopian Northrop F-5As. During August, Ethiopia received substantial numbers of both MiG-21s and MiG-23s, some or all flown by Cuban mercenaries, and two months later claimed to have shot down over 20 Somali MiGs for relatively light losses.

Though bloody and bitter, so-called brush fire wars are seldom

the result of painstaking analysis by major powers. The Vietnam War has been scrutinized by both Mikoyan and the Pentagon. A Department of Defense study examined how the McDonnell F-4B, C, and D Phantom II performed against the MiG-21PF-V.

At first the aircraft were essentially all on the one side, but the conflict escalated. The arrival of the MiG-21PF-V in the NVAF (actually the Air Force of the People's Army of North Vietnam) in spring 1966 quickly resulted in the USAF adding an F-4 fighter escort to all attack missions over the North. The first aerial engagement, on 23 April 1966, was inconclusive, but three days later an F-4C did succeed in destroying a MiG-21. This was attributed to its much more power-

ful radar, with an effective range of 70 km (43.5 miles), and the choice of the heavy medium range AIM-7E Sparrow and close-range Sidewinder AAMs. Provided it worked, the Sparrow proved highly lethal over a range up to 26 km (16 miles) at altitude, falling to 7 km (4.3 miles) near the ground, so the Vietnamese pilots had to work out ways of getting in close.

One battle technique was to use MiG-17s to intercept large formations at low level. This would force enemy formations to climb, at speeds varying from 850 to 900 km/h (528 to 559 mph), or 500 km/h (310 mph) for Douglas A-1 Skyraiders, where MiG-21s in pairs would attack from the rear at 1,200 km/h (745 mph). They would not use their radar, to avoid detection.

MiG-21F-13 534 of the Iraqi Air Force defected to Israel on 16 August 1966. It was evaluated by the Chel Ha'Avir, Israeli Defence Force – Air Force, who could not resist giving it the code number "007" for flight tests! (via Russian Aviation Research Trust)

K-13 (R-3S) missiles would be aimed using their optical sight, and fired when properly locked-on.

In 1967 Soviet observers with the NVAF carried out a careful study and concluded that the NVAF shot down 11 U.S. aircraft and lost nine MiG-17s in the first four months of 1966. From May to the end of the year a total of 47 U.S. aircraft were shot down (confirmed by discovery of the wreckage in almost every case) for the loss of seven MiG-17s and five MiG-21s. In one of the most remarkable encounters, MiG-21 pilot Kha Van Tuke shot down and killed Col D. Folin, commander of a USAF fighter wing, even though the NVAF pilot was alone and surrounded by 36 U.S. aircraft.

If ever an F-4 was unfortunate enough to get into a close dogfight with either a MiG-17 or a MiG-21, it was likely to be in trouble. According to the Mikoyan investigation, in the calendar year 1967 the NVAF shot down 124 U.S. aircraft for the loss of 60 of their own aircraft.

Overall, between 1966 and 1970, the kill/loss ratio in air combat was 3.1:1 in favor of the NVAF, which increasingly used the MiG-21. Over the five years, 32 MiG-21PF-Vs were shot down. In June 1971 U.S. aircraft resumed bombing of North Vietnam, and in spring 1972 a program of 40 well-planned bombing missions called Linebacker-I resulted in intensive combats between F-4s and MiG-21s, the versions involved now being the F-4E and MiG-21MF. By this time the U.S. forces could field just over 1,200 aircraft in the theater, compared with a total NVAF strength of 187, of which in September 1972 only 71 were serviceable, including 31 MiG-21s.

In the first engagement, two MiGs ran into 12 F-4Es and were both shot down. On 27 April, two MiGs encountered a group of F-4s and shot one down. On 6 May four MiGs were met by a formation of F-4s that fired six missiles at a single MiG. The Vietnamese pilot pulled maximum g and survived, only to receive three more missiles, one of which hit; the pilot ejected. Running engagements on 10 May resulted in 15 close dogfights, the result of which was 7-5; the F-4s downed two MiG-21s, two MiG-17s, and a J-6, while the MiG-21s beat three F-4s, the J-6s three and the MiG-17 one. On the following day, 11 May 1972, two MiG-21s acted as decoys, drawing off four F-4Es that were hit from the rear by two MiG-21s that fired three missiles and got two F-4s confirmed. A particularly successful day for the NVAF was 18 May, when MiG-21s flew 26 combat missions, achieved eight combats and shot down four F-4s without loss. In one engagement two MiGs intercepted four F-4s and Capt Egy shot one down with an R-3S fired under high-g in a 90° bank.

Thereafter the honors were roughly even. In an official U.S. statement it was claimed that in July through September 1972 U.S. fighters (of all services) in air combat shot down 17 NVAF fighters (11 MiG-21, four MiG-17 and two J-6) for the loss of 11 F-4s (nine USAF and two USN). The most successful Phantom was the F-4D (seven MiG-21 and two J-6), the F-4E scoring only three MiG-21 and the Navy F-4J one MiG-21 and four MiG-17. Of the 11 MiG-21s shot down, eight were downed by AIM-7 Sparrows and three by AIM-9 Sidewinders (none by guns).

Though U.S. propaganda often tried to give the impression that MiGs could be swatted like flies, their effectiveness is shown by the fact that when President Nixon ordered the Linebacker-II raids by the Boeing B-52 Stratofortress against North Vietnam in December 1972, many of the primary targets of these raids, and supporting missions by General Dynamics F-111s, were MiG airfields.

During these raids there were allegedly two engagements that were never accepted by the other side. On the first day, 18 December, when the targets were the MiG bases of Hoa Lac, Kep and Phuc Yen, a B-52D tail gunner was credited with shooting down a MiG-21, though NVAF records did not show any aircraft as lost on that evening. MiGs, both 17s and 21s, did shadow the bombers even on the darkest nights. The USAF said their task was to report the exact burst height for V750Vk SAMs. The second strange event was that NVAF pilot Pham Tuan became a Hero of the People's Army for shooting down a B-52 on 27 December which the USAF has always attributed to SAMs. He later became the first Vietnamese Cosmonaut.

During Linebacker-II, while the U.S. aircraft could operate from their huge secure air bases and carriers offshore, the MiG-21s had to be airlifted, with their SPRD-99 assisted-takeoff rockets, by Mi-6 helicopters from their destroyed airfields to short, widely dispersed, STOL strips that changed from day to day. The 12 days of this campaign cost the USAF a sobering 31 giant bombers, including 18 shot down over Vietnam. Two were downed by MiG-21s, the second falling on 28 December (the MiG-21 pilot being killed during the attack), but the MiGs were busiest in the daytime. They had eight air combats in which, for the loss of three MiG-21s, they shot down seven U.S. aircraft, including four F-4s and a North American RA-5C Vigilante. In each engagement the NVAF technique was a stern attack and hard break.

During 1972 the NVAF flew 823 sorties, 540 by MiG-21s. A total of 201 air-to-air combats took place, in which U.S. aircraft shot down 54 NVAF aircraft (the NVAF admit losing 48), comprising 36 MiG-21s, one MiG-21US, 12 MiG-17Fs, and five J-6s. They lost 90 of their own number (including 74 F-4s and two RF-4Cs). The MiG-21 score was 67, the MiG-17 11, and the J-6 12.

Yefim Gordon comments, "According to Russian records, which were most carefully compiled, the MiG-21 came out of the Vietnam War better than the F-4. Between 1966 and 1972 U.S. aircraft shot down a total of 54 MiG-21s. In the same period MiG-21s shot down 103 F-4s, and many other aircraft. The F-4s alone lost 206 crew, and of course an F-4 costs more than twice the price of a MiG-21."

MAJOR UPGRADES

In December 1990 the domestic market disappeared. A new partnership led to the formation of the Moscow Aircraft Production Organization (MAPO) in early May 1995. This incorporates the former Factory No. 155 and the big Dementeyev plant that in the 1970s produced 500 fighters per year, and in the 1980s produced 200 MiG-29s per year.

Belyakov and his team took a careful look at the MiG-21. Most customers had very limited budgets, one reason they had invested in MiG-21s. An apparent end to the Cold War had no particular relevance to most of these air forces, who were going to need to update or replace their existing fighters.

Around 1985 Israel's IAI Lavi and Jugoslavia's SOKO Novi Avion ("new aeroplane" – specifically planned as a MiG-21 replacement)

The IAI Lahav Division MiG-21 "production line" in early 1995. While nationality markings are covered up, it is thought that some of the aircraft here – which include three Sparkas – will be Cambodian. In the foreground is the MiG-21-2000 demonstrator/engineering model while in the background is a MiG-23 Flogger that defected to the Israelis. (IAI)

The first MiG-21-2000 demonstration aircraft at the Paris Air Show in 1993. (Robert J. Ruffle)

Another view of the MiG-21-2000 engineering tool/demonstrator, this time at the IAI Lahav Division. (IAI)

had fallen by the wayside. India – the most important export market for the MiG-21 – was still proceeding with its own Light Combat Aircraft (LCA). In addition, the AI Mikoyan team had watched the Chinese emerge as a significant and unwelcome rival for this market, and several other companies or groups had recognized that updating MiG-21s could be good business.

Western avionics firms have been trying with varying degrees of success to get their equipment qualified in various types of MiG-21. The first country actually to carry out an update program was Egypt. When the number of sub-types in Egyptian service had grown to nine, a comprehensive upgrade program was planned. Teledyne Electronics of the USA replaced the SRO-2 IFF installations by its digital TEC-60i, able to handle Soviet and Western frequency bands and interrogation codes. GEC Marconi Avionics won a contract for the Type 956 wide angle HUDWAC, air-data computer and RWR/jammer. Tracor of the USA supplied their popular ALE-40 chaff/flare cartridge dispenser. The Matra 550 Magic 1 missiles were replaced in 1984, first by Sidewinder AIM-9P3 and from 1989 by the AIM-9L. A further 1984 upgrade was to supply for a limited number of aircraft the Italian Elettronica ELT/555 jammer pod, self-powered by a ram-air turbine.

One of the first U.S. companies to reach the contractual stage on upgrades was Grumman (now Northrop Grumman). In January 1987 they signed with the Pakistan Air Force to fit U.S. engines and avionics to both NAMC A-5 Fantans and F-7s, and in August of that year they announced a contract from the US Air Force to design, supply and test new avionics for the Chinese F-8 II. On 21 October 1988 Grumman announced a contract with CATIC to produce an upgrade called the Super-7. They withdrew from collaboration with China in 1989, following the Tiananmen Square massacre.

In 1993, the Pakistan Air Force decided to fit its F-7s with the Italian FIAR Grifo-L multi-mode I/J-band pulse-doppler radar. In France, Dassault Electronique sought MiG-21 upgrade business. It collaborated with Mikoyan and with the Russian state research institute for aviation systems (GoSNIIAS). It devised a total modernization package for the MiG-21, any parts of which can be adopted by customers. The core is EWS-21, a comprehensive threat-warning system. It includes four passive antennas in a fin radome, a processor, night vision goggle (NVG) compatible cockpit display, and a plug-in memory module.

The first MiG-21-2000 on its first flight, 24 May 1995. IAI Lahav Division has transformed an agile aircraft into a formidable one. (IAI)

Two major modification programs have been purely Russian, for the role of pilotless target. One, converting MiG-21PF and PFM aircraft, results in the MiG-21Ye, while the other converts the MiG-21PFM into the M-21. Design work was undertaken in the mid-1960s, with Mikoyan's cooperation, by the Kazan Aeronautical Institute (KAI). Illustrations of the M-21 show two of the several receiver antennae, in the form of truncated cones ahead of and behind the nose gear. There is also a blister above the dorsal fin. These targets follow preset trajectories at subsonic speed, but retain their 7.8 or 8.5g maneuver capability.

The M-21 (*Mishen* – drone) program will ensure that the MiG-21 continues to give faithful service to the VVS well into the next century. The prototype "01" and a former PF was readily identifiable from additional pylon-like structures either side of the rear fuselage at the base of the fin and from a fin-tip fairing. "Production" standard Mishen (example, *Red 03*) have been converted and it is thought that the program involves up to 100 PFs and PFMs. The M-21M had a takeoff weight of 8,400 kg and could operate from dirt runways. The preflight inspection time was 40 minutes; the drone had the altitude envelope from 50 m to 14,400 m, 180 km/h maximum airspeed at 10 to 11 km, 106 minutes endurance, and 8.5 g maximum maneuver load factor. The ejection seats were not dismantled, since every drone was test-flown by a pilot prior to operation.

In early 1996 U.S. company Tracor was offering a drone conversion of the MiG-21, dubbed "QMiG-21" and was reported to be negotiating with three countries (two in the Far East, the other being the UK) over a "womb to tomb" service including ground facilities and engineering. Five MiG-21Rs and a UM had been acquired and were under conversion.

As far as published information is concerned, by 1995 three groups remained in the running to share the MiG-21 upgrade market: IAI and Elbit in Israel, and the MiG-MAPO team themselves. There is no love lost between Moscow and Israel. In 1993 Belyakov exclaimed, "How can anyone offer a MiG-21 update without the cooperation of the designers?" Sadly, it must be recorded that Mr. Belyakov has suffered a stroke, and the de facto head of Mikoyan is today General Designer A. A. Belosvyet. He too is a market-oriented man, determined to compete for the potentially very large MiG-21 upgrade business.

Dealing with Mikoyan's opposition first, Israel Aircraft Industries (IAI), near Tel-Aviv, is a world-class center for upgrading combat jets, principally concerned with avionics and weapons, but also includes a thorough overhaul of every part, and in particular a structural audit. Within a year Lahav had built up a total capability on the later versions,

Dramatically modified cockpit of the MiG-21-2000, dominated by the wide angle HUD, weapons control panel and the new HDD. (IAI)

The first MiG-21-93 on view at the annual display of military weapons at Gorkiy (now Nizhniy Novgorod). The missiles are R-27R (inner pylons) and R-77 (outer pylons), and BVP-30-26 dispensers are scabbed above the wing roots. (Viktor Drushlyakov)

from the MF onwards. Large numbers of aircraft are back in the air, in some cases after they had been grounded for more than five years.

One important upgrade customer was the Romanian Air Force who had approached five countries regarding an upgrade of mainly MiG-21MF and MiG-21bis. Surprisingly, on 24 May 1993 Elbit Ltd, of Haifa in Israel, announced a US$300 million contract with the government to upgrade 100 MiG-21M and 10 MiG-21UM aircraft. Aerostar (prime) collaborated with Elbit (program integrator). The Lancer contract lasted six years. Flight tests were completed on 9 May 1996. Initial program completed in mid-2003. Variants are ground-attack optimized Lancer A (75), Lancer B two-seat trainers (10), and air-defense optimized Lancer C (25).

On 9 October 1998, Aerostar/Elbit began flight tests of a MiG-21bis Fishbed L/N variant upgraded to Lancer III specification accommodating EL/M-2032 radar. This is an export upgrade for the MiG-21 bis, based on the Lancer. New equipment includes:

Elta EL/M-2032M multimode radar (air-to-air version/ Lancer III); Elta EL/M-2001 range radar (air-to-ground version); mission computer; Stores Management System (SMS) Data Transfer System (DTS); Hands On Throttle and Stick (HOTAS); Elbit MultiFunction Color Displays (MFCD); MultiFunction Color Display (MFCD); El-Op HUD/UFCP; DASH helmet and Helmet Sight Tracker (HST); communication system; navigation system (RLG, GPS, DME, VOR/ILS, radio/nav); Horizontal Situation Display (HSD); Computerized Air Data Center (CADC); IFF; chaff/flare dispensers; Radar Warning Receiver (RWR); ECM and health monitoring system.

An Aerofina ejection seat was installed. Weapons include four K-13 Python 3 air-to-air missiles and a variety of bombs including R-60 (AA-8 Aphid), R-13 (AA-2 Atoll) Mk 82, LGB, OPHER Terminal Guidance Unit. The stores pylons are compatible with Western and Eastern armaments including AIM-9 derivatives.

The other firm program for upgrades is that by MAPO-MiG

themselves, in Moscow. The immediate program was to market an aircraft designated MiG-21-93, from the year in which it was first displayed in Moscow. The project got underway because the Indian Air Force (IAF), one of the Mikoyan bureau's best customers and licensees, recognized in the early 1990s that the indigenous LCA was not going to achieve initial operational capability in time. At first, with Mikoyan help, HAL had hoped to update IAF MiG-21s alone. Among other things, they investigated replacing the engines with the Turbo-Union RB.199, General Electric F404, or Soviet Klimov RD-33.

After talking to a number of possible partners, the IAF and HAL decided to accept the proposals of the AI Mikoyan team that only the MiG-21bis version was worth a major upgrade. MiG-MAPO's objective has been to package the radar and weapons of the MiG-29 into the MiG-21bis. The radar offered was the Kopyo (Spear), developed by Fazotron. Like most post-1992 Russian hardware, this has been specially designed as a retrofit for the MiG-21 and other compact fighters. The Kopyo is designed to track-while-scan (TWS) eight targets simultaneously, and lock-on to the two posing the most immediate threat. It incorporates new-generation processors and can be linked with a helmet sight.

At the 1994 Farnborough airshow Phazotron revealed the Super Kopyo. This radar was stated to detect front hemisphere targets at ranges from 57 to 75 km (up to 46.6 miles), or tail-on fighters at up to 45 km (28 miles). It incorporates a new processor, which among other things can count the targets in a group. On 3 May 1994 India's deputy defense minister announced a contract with Sokol and MAPO MiG to upgrade 100 MiG-21bis aircraft with an option for 70 more. That agreement was amended in

MiG-21-93 in the static for the MAKS-95 show, held at Zhukovsky in August 1995. (Yefim Gordon)

1996 to involve 125 aircraft with option for a further 50. At this stage, India also chose to integrate overseas avionics in order to enhance the upgrade (also known as MiG-21I). India also integrated a number of systems from its delayed Light Combat Aircraft (LCA) program.

The first batch was upgraded by Sokol with the remainder by Hindustan Aeronautics Limited following full technology transfer. The first two handed over on 14 December 2000. The aircraft made 300 test flights prior to handover. First HAL example flew in mid-2001, with the upgrades designated MiG-21bis-UPG or MiG-21I completed by 2003.

In June 2003 India announced that 72 of its remaining MiG-21bis would be upgraded with the FK-04 Kopyo radar in a US$300 million contract. The program includes the total replacement of onboard avionics, new canopy, and improved power-generating, fuel, hydraulic, engine control, air conditioning, air

The peacock blue MiG-21-93 cockpit has a multi-function display, HOTAS stick and Zvezda K-37 seat. (Viktor Drushlyakov)

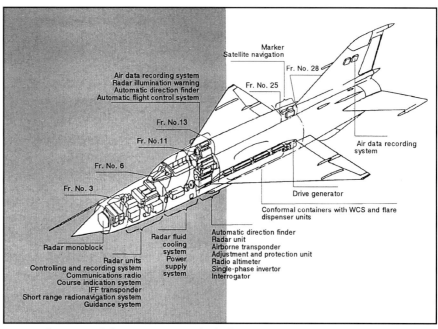

Major elements of the MiG-21-93. (Sokol)

"Production" M-21 drone, Red 03 at NII-VVS. (Yefim Gordon)

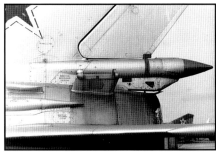

Close up of the pylon at the base of the fin of "production" M-21 drone Red 03. (Yefim Gordon)

The prototype M-21 Mishen drone. Note fin-tip fairing. (Yefim Gordon archive)

Another view of the same drone. (Yefim Gordon)

and liquid cooling, canopy de-icing, and aircraft radar conditioning systems. Systems consist of Phazotron-NIIR Kopyo multifunctional coherent pulse Doppler radar with slot antenna, Sextant Topflight avionics suite with redesigned cockpit, Heads-Up Display (HUD), MultiFunction Display (MFD) as well as Topsight helmet-mounted target designator, Inertial Reference System (IRS), Thales Totem 221G navigation computer, ADU, radio navigation/approach system, communications station, IFF and EW systems from LCA, optional ground-to-air and air-to-air datalink system, and French Video recording system. The Israeli-supplied Radar Warning Receiver (RWR) provides Electronic Counter Measures (ECM) using Israeli-manufactured onboard chaff/flare dispensers. The design of the avionics system provides for integration of the non-Russian systems.

Weapons include the R-60 close-maneuver combat missile with IR-homing warhead; R-73 high-maneuvering combat missile of short- and medium-range with IR-homing warhead; RVV-AE medium-range missile with active radar-homing warhead; R-27 medium-range missile with radar and IR-homing warhead. A ground-attack X-25MP air-radar missile to kill ground and ship radar; KAB-500 correctable air bomb with TV-homing warhead; S-5, S-8, S-24 unguided air rockets; 100 to 500 kg air bomb; GSh-23 built-in gun; countermeasures dispenser system.

In early 1993 Aerea and ANPK MiG (now MIG "MAPO") initiated preliminary discussions on a collaborative program to develop a modular stores carriage system offering a universal system capable of operating both Warsaw Treaty and NATO weapons. In 1995, a collaboration program was announced between Russia and South Africa whereby local industry (Atlas/Denel) might undertake MiG-21 upgrade work for African countries, including the installation of South African avionics.

APPENDIX 1

Exports and Other Upgrades

The very nature of the MiG-21 and its many "clients" works against a really detailed listing of operators, the sub-types, and quantities they have flown. After the country name comes the name of the air arm; MiG-21 types employed; maximum strength thought achieved; status, current numbers operated, etc., plus further notes and details of upgrades. The situation is fluid; please appreciate that this listing is but a "snapshot" in the lifetime of a phenomenal aircraft.

Angolan MiG-21bis parked out and suffering from the elements – note the missing panel from behind the cockpit. Mostly flown by Cubans, the type frequently saw action against rebel and South African forces. (Yefim Gordon collection)

AFGHANISTAN
Afghanistan Army Air Force
Afghan Hauai Quvah
Types: F-13, MF, bis, U, UM
Max strength: 70+
Status: fewer than 10
    operational.

ALBANIA
Albanian People's Army
    Air Force
Types: F-7A
Max strength: 10
Status: Stored in
    operational condition.

ALGERIA
Algerian Air Force
Al Quwwat al Jawwiya
    Al Jaza'eriya
Types: F-13, M, bis, UM
Max strength : 70
Status: Perhaps 36 current.

ANGOLA
Angolan People's Air Force
Força Aérea Populaire de
    Angola
Types: M, MF, bis, U, UM
Max strength: 80+
Status: 23 current

AZERBAIJAN (formerly part of the USSR)
Azerbaijan Air Force
Types: ?
Max strength: 10(?)
Status: 5 operational

BANGLADESH
Bangladesh Air Force
Bangladesh Biman Bahini
Types: MF, U, F-7BG
Max strength: 14, 8 of 16
    F-7BGs ordered in 2005
    had been delivered by mid-
    2006
Status: Perhaps half of the
    MiG-built examples current.

MiG-21MF 201 of the Bangladesh Air Force. Two FAB-100 bombs lie on the table. (Bill Gunston archive)

BELARUS (formerly part of the USSR)
Republic of Belarus Air
    Force VVS
Types: ?
Max strength: ?
Status: Air force established
    1992. Reported one regi-
    ment of MiG-21s.

BOSNIAN SERBIA
Bosnian Serbia Air Force
Types: RF
Max strength : ?
Status: Unknown.

BULGARIA
Bulgarian Air Defense Force
Bulgarski Vozdusny Vojski
Types: F-13, M, PF, PFM,
    R, bis, U, UM
Max strength: 130(?)
Status: 85 current, state
    company, TEREM, began a
    low-cost upgrade of its
    MiG-21bis Fishbed-N in
    2002. The first aircraft was
    flying again by June 2002.

Bulgarian MiG-21RF with white outlined roundels on both the fin and rear fuselage. Callsign number is in white on three-tone camouflage. (Viktor Drushlyakov archive)

BURKINA FASO (formerly Upper Volta)
Burkina Faso Air Force
Force Aérienne de Burkina Faso
Type MF
Max strength: 8 to 12
Status: All withdrawn.

CAMBODIA (formerly Kampuchea)
Cambodian Army Air Force
Types bis, UM
Max strength: 40
Status: Reported 15 extant. IAI upgrade to MiG-21-2000 January 1995. Two batches of nine and eleven MiG-21 bis Fishbed-L respectively. However, this was delayed pending payment, with all nine aircraft held in Israel by 1999. Aircraft still held. Remaining Cambodian examples may be upgraded in China.

Cambodian MiG-21bis line-up. (Cambodian AF via A. J. Walg – Aero Mapho archive)

CHINA
Air Force of the People's Liberation Army
Chung-kuo Shen Min Tai-Fang-Tsun Pu-Tai
Types: F-13, J-7, JJ-7
Max strength: 750-950(?) (J-8 Finback 200?)
Status: 400 J-7 (+100 with Navy), 50 JJ-7

CONGO
Congo Air Force – Force Aérienne Congolaise
Type: MF, U
Max strength: 18(?)
Status: Perhaps 11 current.

CROATIA
Republic of Croatia Air Force
Hrvatske Zracne Snage
Type: MF, RF, bis, UM
Max strength: 28

Status: Perhaps two operational. In September 2002 Aerostar won a contract to upgrade 8 MiG-21bis Fishbed-L and 4 MiG-21UM Mongol-B trainers. First pair delivered on 14 May 2003. The new type designation "D" for "Doradjen," Croatian for "improved."

CUBA
Cuban Air Force - Fuerza Aérea Revolucionaria
Types: F-13, M, MF, PFM, bis, U, UM
Max strength: 174
Status: 150 thought operational.

CZECHOSLOVAKIA & CZECH REPUBLIC
Czechoslovakian Air Force
Cesk Letectvo
Types: F-13, MF, PF, PFM, R, SM, U, UM, US
Max strength: about 450
Status: 35 current, Gripens delivered.

Preserved CS-106 of the markings of the Ceskoslovenské Letectvo (CL – Czechoslovak Air Force). Czech industry made 194 examples. (Russian Aviation Research Trust)

Special markings on Czech Republic MiG-21MF "7711" completely compromises the two-tone camouflage. (Russian Aviation Research Trust)

EAST GERMANY
East German Air Force – Luftstreitkräfte
Types: F-13, MF, PF, PFM, R, SMT, bis, U, UM
Max strength: 240+
Status: United with West Germany. October 1990 – all withdrawn.

MiG-21F-13 of the East German Luftstreitkräfte und Luftverteidigung (Air Force and Air Defence Command) with missile rails, but carrying only a 490-liter tank. (Yefim Gordon archive)

EGYPT
Arab Republic of Egypt Air Force
Al Quwwat al-Jawwia Ilmisriya
Types: F-13, M, MF, PFM, PFS, R, UM, US, F-7B
Max strength: 145+
Status: Perhaps 50 current, upgraded in early 1980s. Included: Teledyne navigation and IFF units, Head-Up Displays by GEC and Tracor ALE-40 chaff/flare dispensers. Weapon system adapted for AIM-9P Sidewinder.

ETHIOPIA
Ethiopian Air Force – Ye Ityiopia Ayer Hayl
Types M, PF, bis, UM
Max strength : 90+
Status: 35, many in disrepair or stored. The three upgrade bids from Elbit/Aerostar (Lancer), Sokol (MiG-21-93) and IAI (MiG-21-2000). An avionics and weapons upgrade for 30 EAF MiG-21 s was expected during 2001, and was understood to be underway in 2003.

FINLAND
Finnish Air Force – Ilmavoimat
Types: F-13, bis, U, UM
Max strength: 61
Status: Replaced with
F-18C/D Hornets.

Finland's Ilmavoimat was one of the first export customers for the MiG-21. The Karelia Wing's Hävittäjäläivue 31 (HäLv – fighter squadron) later re-equipped with the MiG-21bis. (Russian Aviation Research Trust)

MiG-21F-13 MG-35 of the Finnish Air Force. (via Yefim Gordon)

MiG-21bis fighters of the Finnish Air Force have a reduced avionics standard. This is MG-116, of the Karelia wing's HävLv-31. (via Yefim Gordon)

GERMANY
German Air Force – Luftwaffe
Types: MF, PFM, PFS, bis,
U, UM, US
Max strength: ?
Status: In all 251 MiG-21s
taken on. All retired.

With the unification of Germany many former LSK-LV types moved on to serve with the Luftwaffe. As with other "united" German MiG-21s, 23+51 had a short career, being retired by 1992. (Yefim Gordon archive)

GUINEA REPUBLIC
Guinea Air Force – Force
Aérienne de Guinée
Types: ?
Max strength: 7
Status: Unknown, 5 thought
withdrawn.

GUINEA-BISSAU (formerly Portuguese Guinea)
Guinea-Bissau Air Force
Force Aérienne de Guinea-
Bissau
Types: ?
Max strength: around 10
Status: Unknown, 6 (?)
thought operational.

HUNGARY
Hungarian National
Air Defense Group
Magyar Honvédség Repülo
Types: F-13, MF, PF, PFM,
bis, U, UM
Max strength: 120
Status: Upgrade program
not carried through, 56
stored. Gripens ordered.

Wearing the post-WarPac "kite" symbol, Hungarian MiG-21bis Fishbed-N of the Kapos Regiment coming in over the numbers. (Lindsay Peacock)

Red 503 is not a VVS aircraft but an ex-Hungarian Air Force PF imported by the UK aviation film industry specialist Aces High in the spring of 1989 and typical of the many disposals to warbird operators and museums from that time onwards. (Ken Ellis collection)

INDIA
Indian Air Force –
Bharatiya Vayu Sena
Types: F-13, FL, M, PFM, bis,
U, UM
Max strength: 657+
Status: 290. Upgrade
announced for about 120
late 1995, during 1995 10
MiG-21UMs acquired from
Bulgarian and Hungarian
stocks for attrition. HAL
upgrade MiG-21 bis to
MiG-21 bis-UPG.

INDONESIA
Indonesian Air Force
Tentara Nasional
Indonesia-Angkatan Udara
Type: F-13
Max strength: 20
Status: All withdrawn,
mid-1960s.

IRAN
Islamic Republic of Iran
Air Force
Type: F-7M
Max strength: up to 36
Status: Assumed operational,
20 with the Republican
Guard.

IRAQ
Iraqi Air Force
Al Quwwat al-Jawwiya
al-Iraqiya
Types: F-13, MF, PFM, U
Max strength: 80+ (F-7B 75+)
Status: Unknown.

LAOS

Air Force of the People's
Liberation Army
Types: F-13, MF, PF, bis, U
Max strength: 44
Status: 20, plus 6 U. HAL
to refurbish two PFM/bis
late 1997.

*MiG-21bis of the Air Force of the
People's Liberation Army, Laos. Note
up-turned radome covers. (Lao AF via
A. J. Walg – Aero Mapho archive)*

LIBYA

Libyan Arab Jamahiriyah
Air Force
Al Quwwat al-Jawwiya
al-Libiyya
Types: MF, U
Max strength: 94(?)
Status: 50 survivors
thought withdrawn.

MALAGASY (Madagascar)

Malagasy Air Force – Armée
de l'Air Malgache
Types: FL
Max strength: 8
Status: Current?

MALI

Republic of Mali Air Force
Force Aérienne de la
Republique du Mali
Types: ?, U
Max strength: 11
Status: Thought withdrawn.

MONGOLIA

Air Force of the Mongolian
People's Republic
Types: MF, PFM, U?
Max strength: 12+
Status: All withdrawn circa
1993.

MOZAMBIQUE

Mozambique Air Force
Forca Aerea Moçambique
Types: MF, PFM
Max strength: 48+
Status: Perhaps 25.

MYANMAR (previously Burma)

Air Force of Myanmar –
Tamdaw Lay
Type: F-7M, FT-7
Max strength: 36
Status: Deliveries began 1990.

NIGERIA

Nigerian Air Force
Types: MF, U, and 12 F-7NI
and 3 trainers ordered in
2005.
Max strength: 33
Status: Perhaps 16 operational.

*Distinctive with their roundels on the
tailfin, a pair of Aero L-29 Delfins
shield a line-up of five Nigerian Air
Force MiG-21MFs. (via A. J. Walg –
Aero Mapho archive)*

NORTH KOREA

Korean People's Army Air Force
Types: F-13, PF, PFM, U, UM
Max strength: 180+
Status: 147, 30 U.

*Impressive line-up of North Korean
MiG-21PFMs. (via A. J. Walg – Aero
Mapho archive)*

PAKISTAN

Pakistan Air Force –
Pakistan Fiza'ya
Types: F-7P, F-7TP, F-7PG
(66 ordered in 2002)
Max strength: 161
Status: Deliveries began
1991 and continue at
around 12 per year.

POLAND

Polish Air Force – Polskie
Wojska Lotnicze
Types: F-13, M, MF, PF, PFM,
RF, SMT, U
Max strength: 385+
Status: 140 operational

*Removing the seat for servicing from a
MiG-21F-13 of the Polskie Wojska
Lotnicze (PWL – Polish Air Force).
Parked MiG-21s seldom have the
rudder centred. (WAF)*

ROMANIA

Romanian Air Force –
Fortele Aeriene ale Repub-
licii Socialiste Românîa
Types: F-13, FL, MF, PF, U
Max strength: 195
Status: Upgraded to Lancer

RUSSIA – CIS

Air Forces of Russia
Voyenno-Vozdushnyye Sily
Types: MF, PF, RF, SMB, bis,
U, UM
Max strength: 400(?)
Status: Thought withdrawn
from frontline service.
Many late-series examples
still in use for fighter train-
ing, etc. Also M-21 drone
conversion program. Some
CIS states (eg Kazakhstan)
"inherited" MiG-21s but
have not operated them.

SLOVAKIA
Slovakian Air Force
Types: F-13, MF, PF, R, UM
Max strength: 70?
Status: 52.

Unlike the former USSR and Yugoslavia, the dismembering of Czechoslovakia was a peaceful and seemingly straightforward affair. Slovakian MiG-21MF in green/brown camouflage with light blue under surfaces. (Viktor Drushlyakov archive)

SOMALIA
Somalian Aeronautical Corps
Dayuuradaha Xoogga
Dalka Somaliyeed
Types: MF, UM
Max strength: 10
Status: All grounded, wrecked during civil war. Chinese F-7Ms also quoted: unlikely.

SOVIET UNION
Air Force of the Soviet Union
Sovietskaya Voyenno-
Vozdushnyye Sily
Types F-13, MF, PF, PFM, RF, SM, SMB, SMT, ST, bis, U, UM
Max strength 1,200+
Status Azerbaijan, Belarus, Russia and Ukraine have with MiG-21s operational.

SRI LANKA
Sri Lankan Air Force
Type: F-7BS, JJ-7
Max strength: 6
Status: 5 current.

SUDAN
Sudanese Air Force
Silakh al-Jawwiya as-Sudaniya
Types: MF, PF, U, F-7M
Max strength: 18+ (F-7M unknown)
Status: Unknown.

SYRIA
Syrian Arab Air Force
Al Quwwat al-Jawwiya al Arabiya as-Souriya
Types: MF, PFM, bis, U, UM
Max strength: 250+
Status: 220 extant, possible HAL upgrade, TEREM and MiG-MAPO may upgrade 170 aircraft.

TANZANIA
Tanzanian People's Defense Force Air Wing Jeshi la Wanachi la Tanzania
Type: F-7A
Max strength :16
Status: Perhaps 13 operational.

UGANDA
Uganda Army Air Force
Type: MF
Max strength: 12
Status: 5 survivors stored or derelict.

A poor shot, but illustrations of Ugandan MiG-21MFs are very rare. Carnage around an MF, almost certainly at Entebbe. (via A. J. Walg – Aero Mapho archive)

UKRAINE (formerly part of the USSR)
Ukrainian Air Force
Types: SM, bis, U
Max strength: 195
Status: Survivors stored or scrapped.

Cine film frame taken in the 1970s of the first MiG-21s to join the U.S. Air Force at Nellis Air Force Base, Nevada. (via Jay Miller)

A recent photo of a MiG-21UM of Ukraine's air arm. Notice the callsign number in white outline only. (Alfred Matusevich)

VIETNAM
Vietnamese People's Army Air Force
Types: PF-V, PFM, MF, bis, UM
Max strength: 200+
Status: 145

YEMEN
Air Force of Yemen
(North and South, countries merged 1990)
Types: M, PF, bis
Max strength: 70+
Status: All 58 withdrawn, unspecified upgrades reported from MiG/Sokol from 2001.

YUGOSLAVIA
Yugoslavian Air Force
Jugoslovensko Ratno Vazduhoplovstvo
Types: F-13, M, PFM, R, bis
Max strength: 220
Status: About 47 thought on strength.

Night shot of a Yugoslav MiG-21MF. Note the large cover for the PVD boom. (Yefim Gordon archive)

ZAMBIA
Zambian Air Force and
Air Defense Command
Type: MF, U
Max strength: 18
Status: 13

ZIMBAWE
Air Force of Zimbabwe
Type: F-7B or M, JJ-7
Max strength: 48
Status: 14 probably withdrawn

Notes:

- Jordan is reported to have received early F-7Bs and F-7Ms – unconfirmed.
- Slovenia was reported to have had "small stocks" of MiG-21s in mid-1993, but this is also unconfirmed.
- Israel has also operated at least one example.
- United States is known to have evaluated and operated a "small" combat training unit from Nellis AFB.

APPENDIX 2
MiG-21 SCALE MODEL KITS

BY RICHARD MARMO

Ask just about anyone with even a passing interest in aviation what the MiG-21 is and they'll tell you it's a Russian jet fighter. While correct as far as it goes, what many don't know is that it is also one of the most widely exported supersonic jet fighters in aviation history. So much so that it's not uncommon to see MiG-21s wearing the colors of many western nations.

Moving to the model world, the MiG-21 definitely hasn't been ignored. If you browse through *The Collectors Value Guide For Scale Model Plastic Kits* by John Burns (Seventh Edition), some 24 different manufacturers have produced, or reboxed, MiG-21 kits in all of the standard three scales and even a couple of odd-ball scales that make you wonder why they even bothered. Most have been injected styrene, but you can also find vacuform and resin efforts.

If you're interested in adding any of those kits to your collection, good luck. They range from difficult to nearly impossible to find. In fact, a substantial percentage of the manufacturers are those I doubt

many of us have ever heard of. For example: a MiG-21F from Hema (a Starfix rebox) in 1/119 scale, a resin MiG-21R/RF in 1/48 from NKR, and a MiG-21 in an unknown scale from Games. The more familiar names produced MiG-21s as well, notably a 1/72 MiG-21 from Hasegawa, a 1/94(?) MiG-21F from Tamiya, and a very nice 1/32 MiG-21 (with decals for both Russia and North Vietnam) from Revell.

Today, there's still no shortage of MiG-21 kits. All you have to do is pull up the Squadron website, type in "MiG-21," and you're inundated with 85 different listings for the Fishbed. Thirteen are kits in 1/144, 1/72, 1/48, and 1/32. The rest are resin and photoetch detail sets, decals, and publications.

Check out the Stevens International (the exclusive U.S. distributor for Trumpeter) website and you'll find 19 more MiG-21 kits. Granted, there is some duplication, but between Squadron and Stevens International you'll find a grand total of 26 different kits of the MiG-21.

If you build in 1/72, you're fortunate in having a good number to

choose from, including Bilek (reputed to be the best 1/72 offering, though I haven't seen one), Eduard, Fujimi, and Academy. The Academy kit has been around for a long time, is an easy build with minimal parts, looks like a MiG-21 when completed, and is economical at a mere $6.95. It'd be a great starter kit for anyone who's just getting back in the hobby or to get a child started down the modelbuilding path.

As far as 1/48 is concerned, unless there's a rare one hiding in

Looking for a simple starter kit? The 1/72 Academy will do the job, and it's only $6.95.

the bushes or some more kits have been released since this was written, only the KPM, two Academy, and the hard-to-find Revell MiG-21s are available in this scale. Decals are aplenty, but only these four kits. The easiest to find is Academy's pair. And both of them are really quite a nice effort. With lightly engraved panel lines, crisp molding, and a reasonable price of $25 each, I suspect that more than one of these will find their way into many modelers' display cases, especially with some of the truly wild markings that have appeared on aftermarket decal sheets.

An example of the export popularity of the MiG-21 is seen on the Trumpeter Fishbed J boxtop – a Russian MiG in West German markings.

At the present time, this kit is the easiest 1/48 MiG-21 to find. Combine it with some of the wild and wacky markings available on aftermarket sheets and you'll have a real attention getter.

Prefer your MiG on the large side? There's only one game (well, two, if you can track down the old Revell kit) in town and it's the 1/32 scale effort from Trumpeter. In fact, Trumpeter offers six different 1/32 kits, three of them being the Chinese F7 variant of the MiG-21.

Trumpeter's Fishbed J (and presumably the other five as well) has lightly recessed panel lines, a nice cockpit interior that would be even better with the addition of an aftermarket cockpit detail set, metal gear struts, and a metal shock cone that helps keep the nose gear on the ground.

Not only is the box crammed with parts, the aft fuselage can be removed to expose a fully detailed engine. And the aft fuselage itself can be displayed on its own ground trolley. You also get a boarding ladder and a substantial array of underwing stores. Included in the selection are both 800-liter and 490-liter drop tanks, 250 kg bombs, UB-16/UB-32 rocket pods, R-3R/R-3S/RS-2US missiles, and the appropriate wing and centerline pylons. If that isn't enough, you also get four ground crewmen in case you want to create a diorama.

Decals give you a choice of German Luftwaffe or Iraqi markings, but let's not forget all those 1/32 aftermarket decal sheets out there. Price for this Fisbed J – and its five stablemates – is a reasonable $59.98.

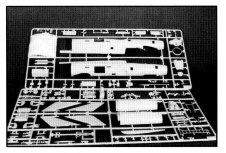

This set of 1/32 sprues deals mainly with the fuselage and cockpit.

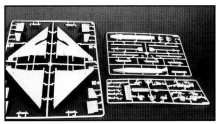

The wings, related parts, and some of the stores are on these three sprues.

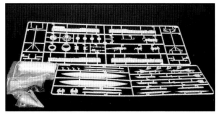

Pylons, engine, and more of the stores are seen here. The bags in the lower left foreground contain the metal gear struts and shock cone.

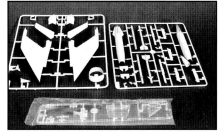

Two more sprues take care of the vertical tail and still more underwing stores. In the foreground is the bag containing the clear parts.

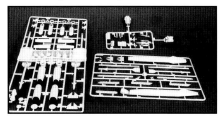

Finally, the rest of the underwing stores.

If you're building up a collection of modern jet fighters, the inclusion of a MiG-21 is an absolute must. And considering its widespread export history, you really should have more than one. With the number of MiG-21 kits available in all four scales, you don't have a reason not to. Do you?

APPENDIX 3 - TECHNICAL DRAWINGS

1/112th scale

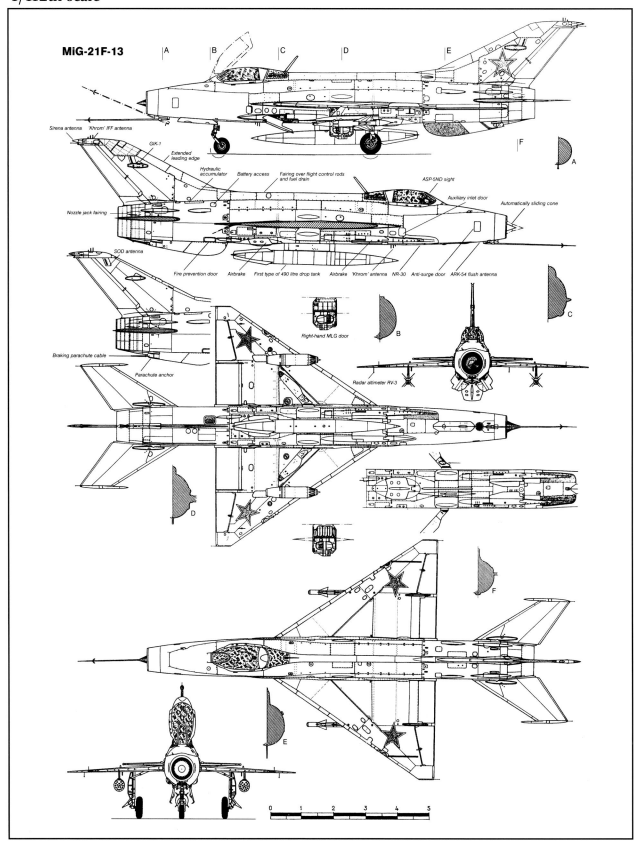

MiG-21F-13

Sirena antenna · 'Khrom' IFF antenna

GIK-1

Extended leading edge

Hydraulic accumulator · Battery access · Fairing over flight control rods and fuel drain

ASP-5ND sight

Auxiliary inlet door

Automatically sliding cone

Nozzle jack fairing

SOD antenna

Fire prevention door · Airbrake · First type of 490 litre drop tank · Airbrake · 'Khrom' antenna · NR-30 · Anti-surge door · ARK-54 flush antenna

Right-hand MLG door

Braking parachute cable

Parachute anchor

Radar altimeter RV-3

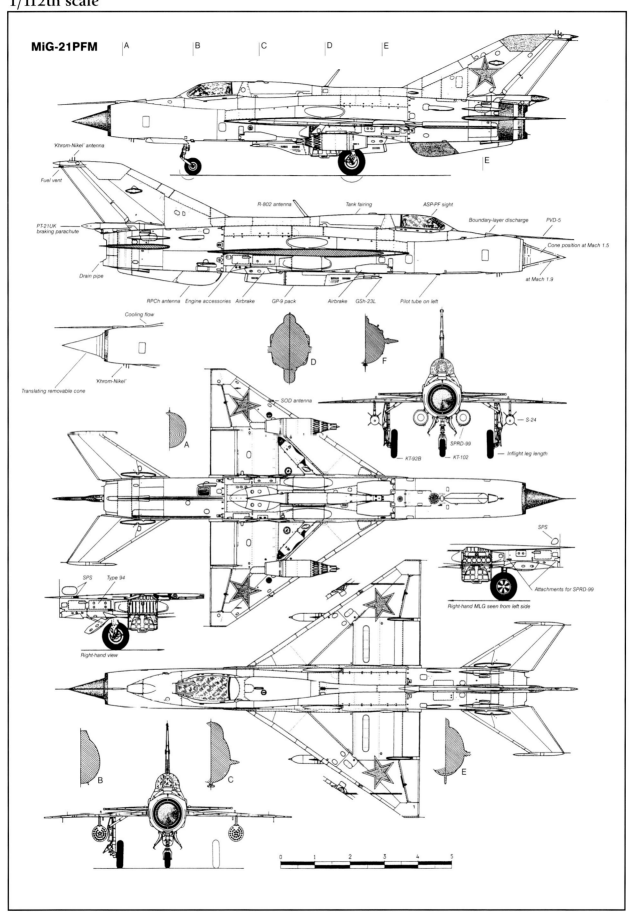

MiG-21PFM

'Khrom-Nikel' antenna

Fuel vent

PT-21UK braking parachute

Drain pipe

RPCh antenna   Engine accessories   Airbrake   GP-9 pack   Airbrake   GSh-23L   Pilot tube on left

R-802 antenna   Tank fairing   ASP-PF sight   Boundary-layer discharge   PVD-5

Cone position at Mach 1.5

at Mach 1.9

Cooling flow

'Khrom-Nikel'

Translating removable cone

SOD antenna

S-24

SPRD-99

KT-92B   KT-102   Inflight leg length

SPS   Type 94

Right-hand view

SPS

Attachments for SPRD-99

Right-hand MLG seen from left side

A   B   C   D   E

D   F   A   B   C   E

0   1   2   3   4   5

1/112th scale

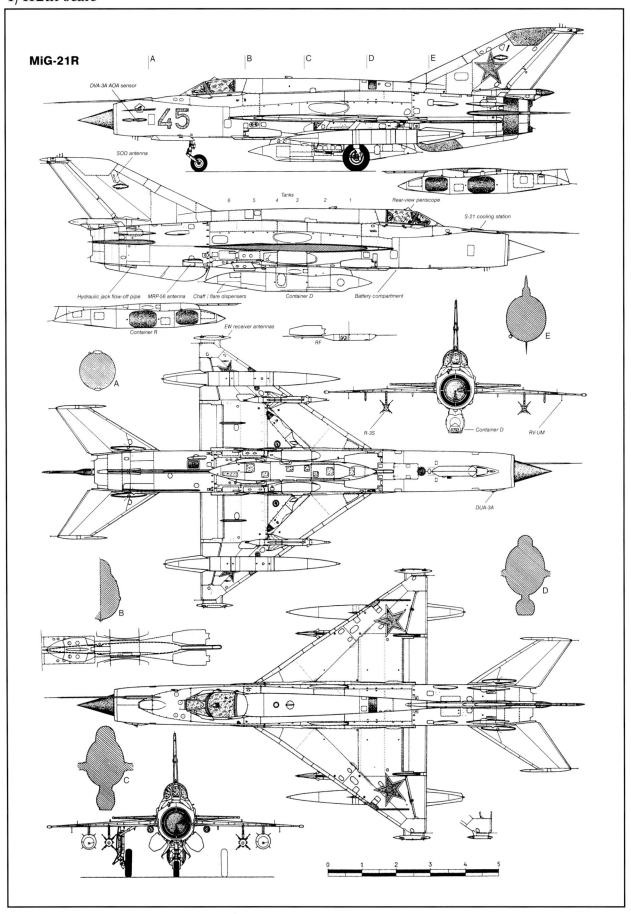

MiG-21R

DVA-3A AOA sensor

SOD antenna

Tanks
6   5   4   3   2   1

Rear-view periscope

S-21 cooling station

Hydraulic jack flow-off pipe   MRP-56 antenna   Chaff / flare dispensers   Container D   Battery compartment

Container R

EW receiver antennas

RF

E

A

R-3S   Container D   RV-UM

DUA-3A

B

D

C

0 1 2 3 4 5

1/112th scale

MiG-21*bis*

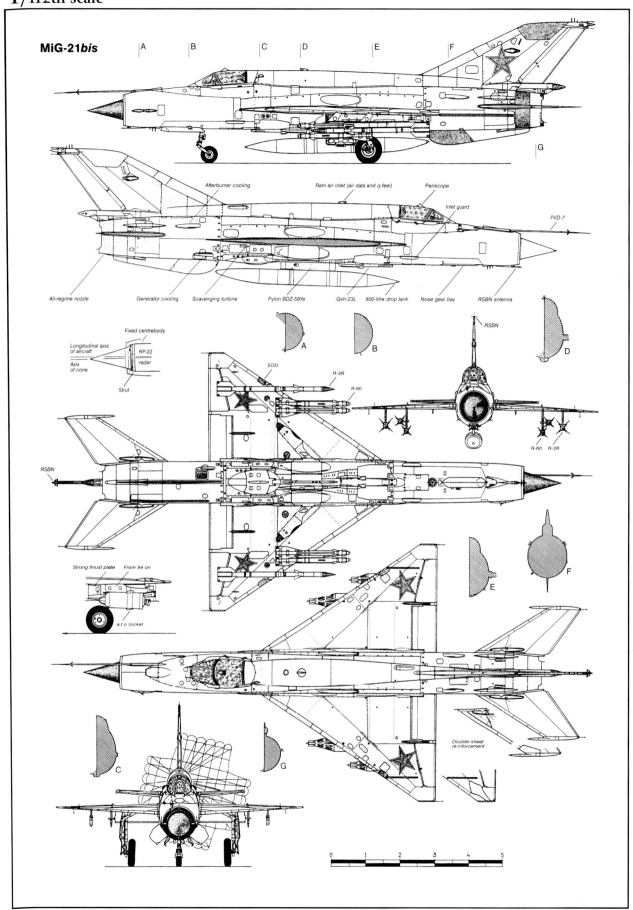

Afterburner cooling
Ram air inlet (air data and q-feel)
Periscope
Inlet guard
PVD-7

All-regime nozzle
Generator cooling
Scavenging turbine
Pylon BDZ-58Ye
Gsh-23L
800-litre drop tank
Nose gear bay
RSBN antenna

A
B
D

Fixed centrebody
Longitudinal axis of aircraft
Axis of cone
RP-22 radar
Strut

SOD
R-3R
R-60
RSBN

R-60 R-3R

RSBN

Strong thrust plate
From 94 on
a.t.o rocket

E
F

Doubler-sheet re-inforcement

C
G

0 1 2 3 4 5

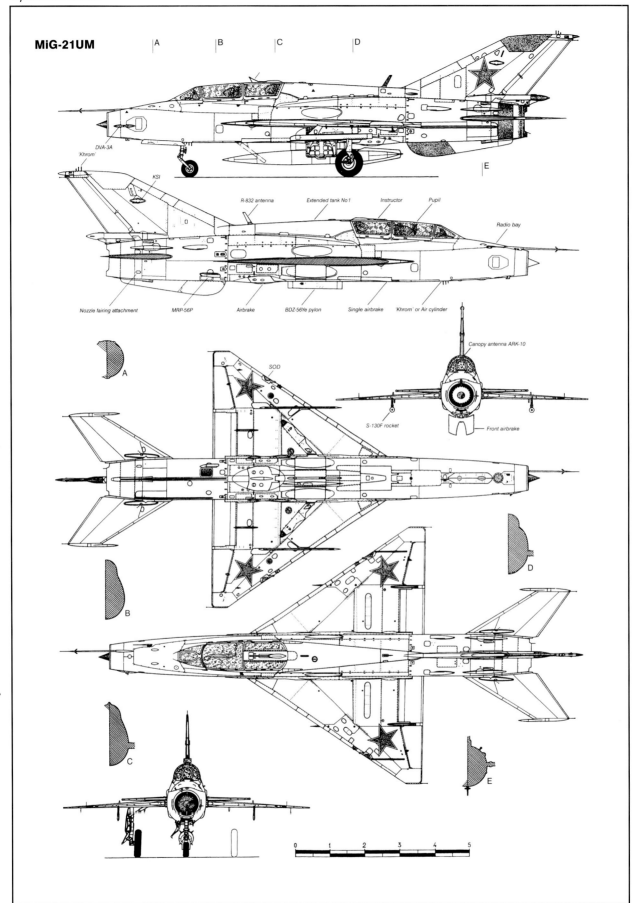

MiG-21UM

A   B   C   D

DVA-3A

'Khrom'

KSI

E

R-832 antenna   Extended tank No1   Instructor   Pupil

Radio bay

Nozzle fairing attachment   MRP-56P   Airbrake   BDZ-56Ye pylon   Single airbrake   'Khrom' or Air cylinder

A

SOD

Canopy antenna ARK-10

S-130F rocket

Front airbrake

B

D

C

E

0   1   2   3   4   5